D1478859

PATRICK WHITE

A TRIBUTE

PATRICK WHITE

A TRIBUTE

Compiled by
Clayton Joyce

An imprint of HarperCollins*Publishers*

AN ANGUS & ROBERTSON BOOK
An imprint of HarperCollinsPublishers

First published in Australia in 1991
This Imprint paperback edition published in 1991 by
CollinsAngus&Robertson Publishers Pty Limited (ACN 009 913 517)
A division of HarperCollinsPublishers (Australia) Pty Limited
4 Eden Park, 31 Waterloo Road, North Ryde, NSW 2113, Australia

William Collins Publishers Ltd
31 View Road, Glenfield, Auckland 10, New Zealand

HarperCollins Publishers Limited
77-85 Fulham Palace Road, London W6 8JB, United Kingdom

National Library of Australia
Cataloguing-in-Publication data:

Patrick White: a tribute

  Bibliography.
  ISBN 0 207 17279 X.

  1. White, Patrick, 1912–1990. 2. Novelists,
  Australian – 20th Century. I. Joyce, Clayton.
  II. White, Patrick, 1912–1990. (Series: Imprint Lives)

A823.3

Cover photo by William Yang
Printed in Australia by Griffin Press

5 4 3 2 1
95 94 93 92 91

PREFACE

I had always hoped that this book would be published during Patrick White's lifetime so that a true picture of his character might be shown through these tributes.

All those who have contributed to this book have done so without payment, with all royalties going to the Patrick White Literary Prize administered by Perpetual Trustees.

Like so many others, I admired from a distance, both the artist and the man. The Australian character was improved by Patrick White's integrity. We would do well to follow his example of generosity and sincerity.

CLAYTON JOYCE

Acknowledgments

Dorothy Green's obituary was originally published in the *Independent* (UK). An earlier version of Humphrey McQueen's tribute appeared in the *Australian Book Review*. Barry Jones's contribution was first published in *Hansard* (9 October 1990) as part of the Parliamentary Tribute to Patrick White. Peter Skrzynecki's poem first appeared in the *Bulletin*, Ray Willbank's essay is from his book *Australian Voices* (University of Texas Press, 1991). Andrew Riemer's appreciation first appeared in the *Sydney Morning Herald* and James Waites' long essay first appeared in the *Independent Monthly* (Australia).

The publishers wish to thank the Patrick White Estate for permission to publish letters, speeches and statements held in this volume, and Jonathon Cape for permission to reprint sections from White's novels.

Clayton Joyce would also like to thank the following: Faith Bandler, Judy Cassab, Lindy Cesar, Marlene Collins, Chandler Coventry, Valerie Davidson, Emanuel De Saxe, Susan Dornan, Leonard French, Silvana Gardner, Kerry Groves, Zhu Jiong-Qiang, Denis Kevans, Colm Kiernan, Paul Knobel, Geoff la Gerche, Jim McClelland, Ward McNally, John Matters, Christina Mimmocchi, Philip Neill, Darcy O'Sullivan, Helen Page, Launa Partlett, Cecily Ryan, Patricia Ryan, Charemaine Seet, Shawn Seet, Siabon Seet, Rae Sexton, Afra Smith, Jennifer Soo, Janice Spencer, Elizabeth Stehlen, Catherine Steward, the staff at Telecom Haymarket Operations, Tom Thompson, Graham Walls and Brett Whiteley.

CONTENTS

DOROTHY GREEN

The death of Patrick White leaves a black hole in the lives of his friends. Some of us felt him to be the touchstone of our actions. Many who did not know him personally will feel they have lost the voice of their country's conscience. It could be said of him as Heine said of himself: '. . . But lay a sword on my bier, for I have been a good soldier in the wars of human liberation.' For more than forty years, first as a writer then as a citizen, White held up a mirror in which he saw himself and his fellow Australians, not only as they were, but as they might be, if they responded to the spiritual as well as the physical challenges of the land they had invaded, and refused to be led like sheep.

White was both visionary and rationalist. He knew that, without vision, the people perish; but he also knew, as his novel *Voss* (1959) demonstrates, that visions based on self-aggrandisement lead to destruction. *Voss* exploded the empty rhetoric extolling Australia as 'the country of the future', by insisting that the future is what is done *now*.

As the 1960s wore into the 1970s, White's faith in his country's future diminished: the present had become too disillusioning. The quality of its political and business leadership was poor and there seemed no hope of bringing about a sense of collective responsibility for the land itself. In *Riders in the Chariot, The Solid Mandala, The Vivisector, The Eye of the Storm* and *A Fringe of Leaves*, the pursuit of integrity became the occupation of the fringe dwellers of society: the simple-minded, the humble and anonymous, the outcasts, the artists, the eccentrics.

The 1970s ended with White's most savage attack on

1

Western consumer society, *The Twyborn Affair* (1979), his finest novel, but oddly enough, one of his most compassionate. Parts of it recall the rich comedy of the early novels, but figures he had lampooned mercilessly in the intervening books were treated with sympathy as well as irony. Unlike his contemporary Barry Humphries, White had humility and a native capacity for self-criticism; he discovered as he grew older that purity of heart and integrity were to be found in unexpected places, even if most often among the powerless.

Nevertheless, his *Credo* (1988) pared religious conviction down to the bare bones of his faith in humanity. As he watched the rot from the top all over the world spreading down the branches of the Tree of Man towards the roots, he grew more and more angry and outspoken. His anger at the betrayal of ideals had its own tradition in Australian writing dating back to the 1840s. It should have come as no surprise that, when goaded by an attack on his own environment in 1972, he suddenly came out of his seclusion, aligned himself with the Builders' Labourers' Union, joined a protest march and spoke from the steps of Sydney Town Hall, calling on his audience to 'protect their parks from political concrete'. The battle which White and his supporters won was against the proposal by the New South Wales government to take over large areas of two historic parks to build an Olympic-size stadium, reducing the city's breathing spaces.

From then on White was in demand as a speaker on numerous public issues. Always an opponent of colonial subservience, he became a convinced republican when the Governor-General in 1975 dismissed the elected Federal Labor government of Gough Whitlam. In 1976 he returned his Order of Australia award and campaigned vigorously for a new Constitution and Australia's independence from both

Britain and America, behaviour which did not endear him to the Bland Society. He regarded himself as an awkward speaker, but the combination of his grave and passionate sincerity and his dry, precise, deliberate speech, punctuated by sudden, sometimes startling colloquialisms, could move even a critical audience to a standing ovation.

Patrick White was born in London during his parents' two-year wedding journey to Europe. They returned to Australia, settled in Sydney near the harbour in a house which figures in several of White's novels. His parents were second cousins, with the same Somerset farming background, the father's side having become wealthy Australian graziers. White went to an exclusive country boarding school, where his 'senses were educated'; then to an English public school, Cheltenham College, 'that expensive prison', which sharpened his conviction of being an outsider. He was a 'colonial' in England and a 'Pom' when he returned to Australia and worked for a while on family sheep stations. He next read Modern Languages at King's College, Cambridge, and travelled widely. After graduation, an allowance from his father enabled him to stay in London and write. By 1941 he had published two novels and a book of verse. During the war he served with the RAF as an intelligence officer in the Middle East, the Western Desert, Egypt, Greece and on the Sudan-Eritrea border.

White was tempted after the war to settle in Greece — his 'other country'; but his longing for the Australian landscape drew him back and exposed him to the anguish of those who accepted as citizens responsibility for their country's mistakes. He was also an artist as well as a citizen and no genuine artist who wishes to write about his country can stay away from it for long. White began his third and first major novel, *The Aunt's Story*, in London, continued it in Alexandria and finished it on board ship returning to Australia in 1948. He settled with his Greek companion of the war years, Manoly Lascaris, on a small farm outside Sydney, where they struggled to grow flowers and vegetables and breed goats and Schnauzer dogs for sale. Here, in spite of recurring attacks of bronchial asthma which plagued him all his life, White wrote three of his finest novels, *The Tree of Man*, *Voss* and *Riders in the Chariots*, and began a fourth, *The Solid Mandala*. In 1964, he and Lascaris moved to Sydney to be closer to friends, to gossip ('the life-blood of a novelist'), to concert halls and theatres. Separately or together, they kept in touch with Greece and Manoly's family, as some of White's best stories reveal.

In his self-portrait *Flaws in the Glass* (1981: the only necessary guide to reading the novels), White disclosed how 'his other country' had given him 'that small Greek of immense moral strength' who had brought equilibrium into a nature 'violent and possessive, jealous, vain and unforgiving'. He had achieved what he envied his parents most, a close, permanent relationship, and with one whom he could trust and respect as well as love. He did not adopt Lascaris's devout Orthodox faith, but it was a star to his 'wandering bark', enabling his creative powers to flow freely.

In an era when social realism in the arts was accepted as the norm, White set out, as Henry Handel Richardson had done before him, to re-examine the nature of realism, to question the apparent opposition between the flesh and the spirit. The impulse may have come from Johnson's *Rasselas* as the explicit allusions in *The Aunt's Story* and the title of a lost play, *Return to Abyssinia* indicate. He ranged more widely than any other Australian novelist over the social spectrum from wealthy property-owners to derelicts — an endless gallery of figures with each of whom he had an extra-

ordinary empathy, endowing even walk-on characters
with momentary life.

White said he became a novelist because he was a
frustrated actor, 'as a means of introducing to a dis-
believing audience the cast of contradictory characters
of which I am composed'. If he railed against hypocrisy
and greed, it was because he understood their temp-
tations. Keats's definition of the true artist fitted White
exactly: 'What shocks the virtuous philosopher,
delights the [chameleon] poet.'

In *Memoirs of the Many in One* (1986) White satirises
with great glee the 'transcendentalist' critics who tried
to fit him into their categories. But it needs to be read
in the light of *Three Uneasy Pieces*, which was rushed out
in 1987 to avoid the Bicentenary. The last pages
illustrate the continuity of his convictions.

In 1973, White was awarded the Nobel Prize for
Literature, an event which robbed him of his privacy
for good. With characteristic generosity (and perverse
irony?) he gave away the prize-money to endow an
annual Patrick White Prize for authors who had
received less attention than they deserved. Equally
generous was his encouragement of young writers, not
to mention his gifts of fine paintings to the New South
Wales Art Gallery, which, he said later, kept most of
them in the basement.

The Nobel Prize gave rise to misconceptions abroad:
that White was the only writer of importance Australia
had produced; that there had been no symbolic or
metaphysical writers before him; and that he had
'introduced a whole new continent' to world
literature. The truth is otherwise on all three counts,
especially the second. White's was the crowning
achievement of a long spiritual tradition, strange as
this may seem to the British fans of Barry Humphries.

In an age of moral relativism, his belief in absolutes
seemed an anachronism. His love of country was one

of these, as defined by Richard Aldington: 'Patriotism is a lively sense of collective responsibility. Nationalism is a silly cock crowing on its own dung-hill.' In a world given over to destructive nationalism, Patrick White's life stands out like a beacon.

MANNING CLARK

Patrick White was one of the few people I have met who belongs to a different order of being. Perhaps that was why we ordinary human beings felt so inadequate in his presence. We were not capable of responding to his needs: we therefore must have let him down. Perhaps that is also why he denounced us all from time to time with all the fury and the passion of an Old Testament prophet.

There was another man inside Patrick White — the man with the vision of a great artist. That man illustrates the point made by Sigmund Freud about Michelangelo's sculpture of Moses: the test for a man is whether he can channel the passions aroused by the worshippers of the Golden Calf into works of creation. It is easy to give way to anger. Only those whose eye is single, those endowed with a higher order of being can work the great marvel of changing the dross of anger into the gold of great art. That is what Patrick White achieved in such works as *The Aunt's Story, The Tree of Man, The Solid Mandala, The Ham Funeral* and many other works. The anger was expressed too in the public speeches, the interviews in the press and on radio, and in conversations with friends.

We are all the beneficiaries of his great gifts. There are from time to time human beings who have taken such a huge bite at the fruit of the tree of knowledge that they have become gods. Patrick White was one of them. That was neither easy for him nor for us. His work will tell those who come after us that in an era enslaved to greed and titillation there was at least one mighty spirit in the land.

EDMUND CAMPION

Like all of us, Patrick White is dying. When he dies, I predict there will be a torrent of vindictive stories about this sacred monster of Australian literature. Like that other sacred monster of literature, Evelyn Waugh, White has been all his life a spitting blue-tongue lizard whose victims are legion. The literary world seethes with stories of his enormities; and, once the master is safely dead, these stories are likely to become public property.

So, before that time, let me enter a plea for the defence. In Russian folklore there is a tale of a crabby old woman who died and was plunged into the Lake of Eternal Forgetting. 'Help,' she cried, 'get me out of here.' The Angel of Mercy, passing by, heard her cry and asked, 'Did you do one good thing in your lifetime?' The woman considered: 'Yes,' she said, 'I once gave a beggar a spring onion.' So the Angel of Mercy took a spring onion and lowered it down into the Lake of Eternal Forgetting and drew the crabby old woman out. This, then, is the story of Patrick White's spring onion which, against all the stories of his awfulness, should be enough to save him from the Lake of Eternal Forgetting.

Twenty-five years ago he and his companion, Manoly Lascaris, lived on a six acre farm at Castle Hill to the west of Sydney. Already his novels *The Tree of Man*, *Voss* and *Riders in the Chariot* had begun to win acclaim for him. His plays had been less successful, although White seemed to want to persevere with the theatre. An intensely private person, he kept out of the public eye.

So it was something of a surprise when he agreed to

meet two dozen young Christian Brothers, just out of training and about to start teaching. The young brothers went to Castle Hill on a January afternoon with their Master of Scholastics, Brother G. C. Davy, a cultivated man.

White showed them through the 'Dogwoods' homestead, allowing them time to appreciate his pictures. They were surprised to find that he was an avid collector. The walls seemed crowded with paintings: three Sidney Nolans, Roy De Maistre, John Coburn, Dickerson, Gleghorn, Gleeson, Fairweather, Perceval . . . it was a stunning assemblage of contemporary Australian art. He told them he liked to chance his arm with living Australian painters, rather than buy artists with settled reputations. Greek icons gave another dimension to the art on the walls.

Going through the house, the Brothers noticed how spick and span the two bachelors kept everything. They were led outside, where afternoon tea, with several Greek dishes, was laid on a table under the trees.

Then it was time for talk. Patrick White told the Brothers how he wrote his novels, starting with the characters who grew in his mind until they found a story they were able to inhabit. He said he didn't 'enjoy' writing, it was more of a personal compulsion. Here Manoly Lascaris chimed in with the information that the novelist sometimes spent weeks polishing a single phrase. When he flagged he sought refreshment in music. Although later novels had greater commercial success, he thought his best novel to date was *The Aunt's Story* (1948). He claimed not to read much fiction.

Patrick White showed exquisite courtesy to his at times gauche questioners. No, he had had few associations with Catholics, although he observed them closely. No, he had not made a special study of

Aboriginal psychology; indeed, he had never met an Aborigine. What did he think of A. D. Hope's charge that he wrote 'illiterate verbal sludge'? He smiled faintly but, Brother Davy thought, tolerantly.

Where are they now, those two dozen young Christian Brothers who sat at the feet of Patrick White twenty-five years ago? I wonder if they still remember his unusual grace and generosity of spirit at afternoon tea. I'm sure the Angel of Mercy hasn't forgotten it.

JUDITH WRIGHT

Patrick White's name first reached me on a second-hand stall in Sydney, about 1942. It was on a copy of *Happy Valley*, moderately ill-used and picked up for a couple of shillings. I've lost it, or someone has relieved me of it, over the years. I read it then with a deep curiosity; was it possible to write about an Australian country town, such as I had come from, to make the writing valid and even to publish such a novel overseas? That was the ultimate accolade for an Australian writer then.

Yes, I decided, the novel did work and was impressive. But though I myself wanted to be a writer, had gone to university to add something to my qualifications to be one, and was writing poems and planning a novel of my own, the war and its demands intervened. It sent me back to the country where I had been born and bred, to help my father on his station since most of his other helpers had been snatched into the Forces.

There I learned that the Patrick White whose book I had bought was a kind of connection of my own, in the way in which most country families then were connected with, knew, or knew of each other. Those families, their roots maybe only a couple of generations deep, inherited a bond from early days, when 'conquering the country' involved mutual co-operation — whether in driving off the original inhabitants, in tide-over loans or patronage or intermarriage or shared knowledge. Those memories and relationships kept their fortunes connected.

But about Patrick White (a few years older than I) and his immediate family not much was known. In some way they were not quite 'us'; Patrick's mother lived, not on the family property, but in Sydney (my country housewife relatives clucked enviously perhaps). As for Patrick himself, he had been sent to school in England, ignoring the public schools of the local aristocracy. The word 'stuck-up' was implied if not mentioned. As to the novel, nobody else in my surroundings had read it (indeed, an Australian novel was a rarity in their bookshelves).

But the Whites — everyone knew them. A long-established pastoral family, they had begun their Australian story in the Hunter Valley as most of my own family connections had done; the New England branch had 'stately homes' near Armidale, my Wright great-grandmother had built her own retirement house near Booloominbah; the Misses White and their father and their family were essential to every important event or committee in New England.

But the name, and the book, stuck in my mind. I too was a dissident from that sheepfold, a country-bred descendant of country people who had slipped out of the net. (Merely to go to university, especially for a woman, was enough to make me, too, a 'stuck-up' person.) My family went back a long way into Australia's very shallow past; to be able to call oneself a 'fifth-generation Australian' as I did, was still a rare distinction. But almost nobody I knew had dreamed of going to university. The land, such large gobbets of it as our forebears had taken, was enough for my generation — and indeed for the next.

I knew the New England Whites and their 'grand houses' in my hated schooldays. I was one of the schoolgirls, stiff, spotty and embarrassed, who were sometimes asked in batches to afternoon tea on the lawns of Booloominbah and Saumarez on Sundays and holidays. I'd rebelled against that patronage, the gloves and stockings and good manners and gentility it seemed to entail. It was no recommendation, in my eyes, for Patrick's novels.

I heard nothing of Patrick and his writing at those tea-parties. Nor, when I went back in wartime, were such matters discussed. I did not find a copy of Patrick's next book, *The Living and the Dead*, for years to come. Books published in England in the early years of the war were nearly impossible to get. But at the end of the 1940s, by which time I was living in Queensland, I found *The Aunt's Story*, and was even more impressed. Though Australia was only its starting point, so to speak — (and it was Australia, I knew, that I had to accept as my main theme) Theodora's travels struck a nerve. I too had gone to England and Europe in 1937, and had struggled with the terrors of those times and the approaching darkness, clearly then not far ahead. Dissociation of lives, madness, uprootedness, were part of my own times.

But I was not a novelist. I had destroyed the half-finished novel written in New England in the 1940s and since then I had been writing poetry and a few short stories; to get enough time and leisure to work on a full-time job like a novel seemed impossible, especially for a woman with a need to earn a living. Grants under the old Commonwealth Literary Fund were few and far between and to get one, one practically had to have a novel already published (a kind of double-bind that probably kept many people from writing at all). But I had been lucky. Increasingly deaf and impatient with my job, when the war ended I had decided to leave my statistical work and work instead on my grandfather's diaries, for a kind of fictionalised biography. I had published just about enough to score a year's support grant. Those diaries were very authentically Australian; if I wanted to interpret the country's history, they were a clear path into it. For me the landscape I knew was full of a deep and urgent meaning. I had already felt the problem of identifying with my family's past here and their effects on the land they took. These hills and plains, these rivers and plants and animals were what I had to work with as a writer, and they themselves contained the hidden depths of a past beyond anything that cities and the history of the British invasion had to offer. So, after I had finished *The Generations of Men* and sent it with increasing despair to publisher after publisher, and put it away in favour of other things including my family (a daughter born in 1950 and a husband often ill from service in World War I, with his own urgent work to do), I read *The Tree of Man* with a deep recognition. Somehow it bolstered what I had been trying to do.

In 1957 Patrick published *Voss*. My admiration for that feat of arms against the establishment views in which we had been born, and for its illumination of the story of the European mind in its meeting with the country, made me feel that Patrick, even in his long absence from Australia, knew it deeply. And he and Manoly moved into the city, the themes changed. The Cold War, its deliberate nastinesses, its hypocrisies and hidden or overt threats to any who thought differently from the dumb majority, had probably driven others of my generation into retreat and silence, or into looking for support in Jungian psychology and for hope in European philosophers and art. The 1950s saw the beginning of such retreats — the poetry of Australians at that time became more reclusive, more defensive, less ambitious. McAuley turned Catholic, Kenneth Mackenzie died in a river, Joan Mas in a bay, and more writers seemed to be going overseas. That Patrick had come back, was writing here, and was not rejecting Australia for Abroad, meant a great deal.

So from *Riders in the Chariot* onward through the rest of the great city novels, he was interpreting a different

Australia from that of *Voss*, but certainly one I was living in, though far from Sydney. The city, that increasingly multinational complex of themes and people and crude politics, was an international symbol as well as a national one. It was not my arena, but through it came the increasingly destructive influences that were despoiling the world. I was watching, with increasing distress and horror, not only the terrible building up of the great weaponry of the Cold War, but the effects of the technological and industrial invasion of the land I loved.

I felt I had to move into that arena, if only to try to rescue something of what I loved from the new materialism, the dollar-minds and the ugly politics of the time. Whatever bonds Australians had slowly begun to forge against their early fear and hatred of the land and its original peoples seemed to be endangered. I was part of a kind of resistance movement, called conservation; and was now seen as politicised, less a writer than a supporter of hopeless and reactionary causes.

For a time, Patrick had seemed to be above that battle, working steadily along his own lines. I remember a short correspondence we had (over the miners' attack on Fraser Island perhaps) when I had told him a little of how I felt about his work and the importance of his remaining a writer — not, as I was, too harassed and driven by that battle to concentrate on writing. But when the monsters attacked his own arena and Centennial Park was at stake, he too was leading the protest; and when he published the 'Fraser Island novels' (I think of *The Eye of the Storm* as well as *A Fringe of Leaves* as essentially emerging from his visit to that lovely threatened island) I was a hopeless addict once again.

Since then Patrick and I shared platforms from time to time: in 1974 for the Whitlam vision; in 1975 to farewell and mourn it; over the fight for peace and sanity and against the Bomb and the pusillanimity of a 'Labor' government on uranium mining . . . In fact, we seldom met except on such occasions. But since our background is a shared one, and our stories have something in common above and beyond that, I think we have had a bond of continuity. Both of us stemmed from days when the Australian tale was just beginning, with all its uneasy European legacy, its own contribution of blood and ugliness, and its struggle towards understanding. That so great a writer has emerged from that background can't help but give me hope that we're after all redeemable.

NICHOLAS HASLUCK

Now and again during the years in which my father was in office as Governor-General my wife and I left Perth to spend a few weeks at Admiralty House in Sydney. What a strange, Cinderella-like experience it was to quit our suburban existence for a while, the daily round of living and working in an outlying centre, and be miraculously transformed into two spruced-up figures rubbing shoulders with cabinet ministers, judges, chiefs of staff and foreign emissaries, knowing that all too quickly the gaiety and glitter would evaporate, and we would be returned to our pumpkin surroundings again. So be it. Gather ye rosebuds while ye may. We plunged into the new milieu with gusto.

Unlike his predecessors, my father, a writer himself, liked to keep in touch with what was happening in the literary world. On one of our visits to the East I was thrilled to discover that the guest list for a forthcoming dinner party was weighted in favour of well-known Australian writers: Patrick White, Kenneth Slessor, Douglas Stewart, Grace Perry, David Malouf, Nancy Keesing, Geoffrey Lehmann and many others.

When I entered the living room at Admiralty House I looked around expectantly, but, as happens so often in a room crowded with tuxedo-clad men and glamorous women, it was difficult, at a first glance, to sort out who was who. An aide-de-camp whisked my wife away. Adrift, I attached myself to two silver-headed men talking earnestly in a corner of the room one of whom I knew to be Grace Perry's husband, a distinguished surgeon. I took the other man to be the spouse of someone else — the black tie and starched shirt gave him the look of a merchant banker — and while they

17

talked, gossiping in a manly way about shark sightings in the Hawkesbury River, I surveyed the scene cautiously. Where were the famous writers?

The minutes were ticking by. The two fellows at my elbow seemed pleasant enough, and the conversation about the sharks was mildly interesting, but time was precious. At the end of the week the clock would strike and I would be dumped back at my desk in Perth to deal with the same old heap of legal files, most of them rendered even more intractable than usual by three weeks of neglect. I began to fidget. I had to find me a writer before the evening expired.

At that moment one of the aides joined our group, introduced me to the silver-headed figure at my elbow — Kenneth Slessor — and moved me on. Outside in the dark the harbour waters between Pinchgut and the shadowy bridge shone with deep and dissolving verticals of light, but I, the unobservant one, had lost my chance to talk to the man who had coined those magical lines. What would happen next I wondered?

It was then that I was introduced to Patrick White, he at least being recognisable. Determined not to let this opportunity slip, I ventured a few remarks, a few more (was his attention wandering?), and finally, bereft of inspiration, panicking, I began talking about sharks in the Hawkesbury, the fact that more had been seen of late.

The listener's grey eyes were upon me, observing, absorbing, measuring. As I stumbled onwards, I detected a slight wincing, a sense of withdrawal, as though each superficial comment had touched a nerve somewhere and inflicted pain. Fortunately, at that moment an announcement was made and we all moved into the dining room. I had been with him for not more than a few minutes, and he had scarcely uttered a word, but I was left with an uncanny feeling that he had seen right through me. An unspoken query seemed to be hovering behind the faintly affronted expression: 'I can hear the words you insist on uttering, but what are you really saying?'

After dinner, while the guests were still seated at the long table, discussion turned to Norman Lindsay — his versatility, his influence, the need to commemorate the richness of his artistic life. Of those present, Slessor and Douglas Stewart were Lindsay's closest friends, and it was fascinating to hear the idea begin to take shape around the table that a trust should be constituted to preserve Springwood, Norman Lindsay's home in the Blue Mountains, as a testimonial to his life and work. The discussion was rounded off by Douglas Stewart rising to his feet to make an impromptu speech in which he undertook to carry forward the proposal, as indeed he did, so that Lindsay's house and studio in its secluded bushland setting is now open to visitors.

Patrick White said little during the discussion and one imagines that, in the normal course, such exchanges, foreshadowing meetings and committee work to come, would be quite foreign to his disposition. But the point is: he was there. A friend of mine once said that one of the most important events of the post-war era as far as Australian writers are concerned, more important than financial support from governments or the setting up and consolidation of various literary organisations, was the fact that Patrick White chose to come back to his native land. A great and dedicated artist, working at the height of his powers for many years, becomes, by his presence alone, a force for creativity, an encouragement to those toiling on the slopes below. Much the same thought was expressed in the discussion that evening concerning Norman Lindsay.

About eight years earlier, while completing a law degree in England, I arranged to meet my mother in

Greece for a two-week holiday. She had just finished one of her many books and was in need of a rest, she said. At the time I received her letter I had just handed in yet another university assignment and felt the same. In due course we met as planned and, two or three days later, having caught our breath, we were invited to call on the Australian ambassador.

The ambassador had another visitor that day. The woman sitting opposite us in the tiny reception area was small and dumpy and clad in an ill-fitting pink floral dress. Her eyes, cast downwards, were invisible beneath the brim of a large straw hat. She was clearly an Australian traveller like ourselves but to engage her in conversation was impossible. She sat staring at the old shopping bag at her feet and seemed lost in a world on her own.

'That's Eve Langley,' my mother whispered. 'The writer!' Her tone of voice conveyed her sense of respect for the woman nearby, and some echo of that tone has stayed with me ever since. That is why the presence of a Patrick White in our midst has been so important. A tone. A glance. A whisper. To an impressionable mind, such signals mean more than a distant accolade or a textbook full of learned articles.

It may be that a similar nuance in my mother's voice struck a chord with White himself. Not long after the dinner party I have described he sent my mother a recent issue of a magazine published in New York called *Prose*. Many years have gone by since my mother was an active writer and, owing to age and frailty, she is no longer in her own home. The magazine stands on my shelves now. It has a sheet of notepaper in it, written in my mother's hand, which reads: 'This magazine was sent to me by Patrick White because of a talk we had on Edith Wharton once at a dinner party at Admiralty House this year, 1974. I replied thanking him.'

Some years later I saw Patrick White at close quarters again, but in quite different circumstances. I had become a part-time member of the Australia Council. When appointed I assumed, naively as it turned out, that I would be spending most of my time talking enthusiastically about artistic matters. The world doesn't work that way. The presumption is that the man with the law degree likes to talk about legal and financial problems. I finished up on a management committee, wielding a pocket-calculator, trying to persuade my colleagues to take an interest in the budget. Fortunately, the committee included a lively Brisbane businessman, Brian Sweeney, who was also chairman of the Theatre Board. We soon slipped into a pattern, once the day's work was done, of heading off to the theatre, ostensibly to appraise the quality of various productions, but in fact to have some fun.

Brian was outgoing and gregarious, and liked to go backstage after the performance laden with champagne. I became the champagne carrier, and dispenser too — a kind of effervescent Gunga Din. Within minutes of the curtain falling there we would be, Brian hammering on the dressing-room door, me nursing the carton of fizz. Brian seemed to know everyone and, on the whole, our visits appeared to be welcome, although, for my part, I was largely occupied with popping corks and juggling plastic cups.

One night we went to see the Louis Nowra play *Visions* produced by the short-lived Paris Theatre Company in a theatre opposite Hyde Park. We arrived backstage, gift-laden as usual, to find that Patrick White was amongst the well-wishers who had turned up to pay their respects to the cast, a fine group of actors which included Kate Fitzpatrick and John Gaden.

The dressing room was small and crowded. 'What did you think of it?' someone in the cast asked a visitor.

'Let's hear the chairman's verdict,' the visitor replied, neatly sidestepping the question. Sweeney was equally adroit. 'There's the man to ask', he declared, as all eyes swivelled in my direction, the champagne charlie at the end of the room.

'It was . . . interesting,' I said, lamely. I had enjoyed the show very much but in the unfamiliar backstage world was afflicted by the age-old problem of how to say so. 'I liked it. I really did. I mean it. I'm not just saying that . . . ' The words, the inadequate utterance, petered out. I was conscious that a mood of despondency had descended. Was it just my imagination or did I see Patrick White in the far corner wincing again?

'Don't do that to me,' I hissed at Sweeney, *sotto voce*, as the champagne was passed around to revive the spirits of those present. Responding to questions from a room full of lawyers about the difficulties of the Paddington Town Hall trust was far easier, I concluded, than to express an opinion to a gathering of anxious actors within minutes of the final curtain. Geoffrey Lehmann once told me that if Kenneth Slessor was ever asked to comment on a young poet's work his criticism invariably fell within one of three categories 'Good', 'Very good', or 'Brilliant'. I can see why, and I can also see why the chairman of the Theatre Board chose to assert his authority via the muzzle of a champagne bottle.

I lack the skill to try and sum up Patrick White's achievement. I read his works for pleasure. What strikes me principally is the sense of scarifying honesty, of insight. 'Yes, that's how it is,' one murmurs, sentence by sentence as the book proceeds. He cuts away the dross, the platitudes, the banalities, the vacuous utterances. As my brief encounters with the man himself suggest he reacts quickly to whatever is superficial and insincere. He gets down to bedrock, to what matters, and this is true especially of my favourite work, *The Twyborn Affair*. The fact that it was written late in his career, like his decision to return to Australia, is bound to encourage other writers to press on.

Recently, while writing a novel called *The Country Without Music* in which various musical motifs have a part to play in the structure of the work, I happened to pick up the magazine *Prose* which Patrick White sent to my mother so many years ago. The issue in question contains an essay by John Hollander bearing the title 'The Music of Silence'. The essay incorporates a quotation from Montaigne who remarked that the music of the spheres, if actual, would be inaudible in any event because of its continuous presence to which habit would dull our ears. The thought was exactly what I wanted. I used it. In a host of tiny ways, most of them invisible to the outside world, a great writer such as Patrick White was bound to have, and has had, an enduring influence on those around him. That is part of his achievement.

ROBIN WALLACE-CRABBE

In the late 1970s down on the Monaro there was a story going round about the tour of the region Patrick White had made. His guide was David Campbell who had his own tale to tell of being invited to dinner at Patrick White's house, of preparing himself for demanding literary conversation then finding things were not to be like that at all. More fun, less heavy work.

I seem to remember there was a great deal of Patrick White conversation in the south-east of New South Wales at that time. The story of the White visit to the region may have developed with the telling, how would I know? It was generally assumed that he'd been redeveloping a sense of what this cold hard country is like. And maybe at the same time getting off on the smell of mutton fat, the vistas of lichen-coloured rocks, frostbitten grass, erosion, rabbit-warrens, and the decaying grandeur of those isolated homesteads. White was, we are told, fed and bedded down for the night in various houses, his gracious hosts having brushed up on the content of his books so that conversation might flow. Proper. First to the right and then to the left . . . or is it the other way around?

A second instalment of the Monaro story, this I expect even more fanciful than the first, has the same hosts waiting with bated breath for *The Twyborn Affair* to appear, so they might pore over the text in an endeavour to spot themselves or their spreads. How would they be depicted? Maybe the prize rams might get a guernsey. Would they like what they read? The people, that is, not the sheep.

Interesting questions. And worth asking. For one

could be excused for thinking that these good folk might not be pleased with what they read.

It was hard to avoid the idea, perhaps it still persists, that in certain elevated quarters Patrick White was regarded as a class traitor.

Which was interesting for me because when I had been a young artist in Melbourne I spent a lot of my time with Communists. Today, of course, it seems that history has shat on the Communists. History started to run the wrong way for them from the time of the Russian invasion of Hungary. But I don't want to disown my association with those people because, all considerably older than me, at that time they clung to the idea that large chunks of the Right of politics had recently been soft on Hitler. The people I met at the time reckoned they were shoring up attitudes so the world might avoid the possibility of another Hitler. Generally these Communists, my Communists if you like, were concerned about justice and social equality. No need to scorn them for that. And they were staunch opponents of racism in a frighteningly racist Melbourne.

This was a time when people were deserting the party. I am talking about, say 1957 to 1965. I remember spending a day with a couple of these Communists, discussing the work of Patrick White. At issue was whether he was good enough for a certain magazine to run an article on him. The argument against his being included was that his work placed too much emphasis on the individual, that the values one found in his books were in essence bourgeois ones.

Sounds a long time ago that, right?

But it happened. I remember because I argued the other way. This didn't carry a lot of weight because I was so much younger than the others. And never a party member. Not the joining type, see. Malleable perhaps . . . but.

Looking back I don't believe there were too many of the proletariat involved in such discussions. When it came to real strikes, to bringing shipping to a standstill, a book like *Voss* was no big deal one way or the other.

So, in those . . . when did *Voss* come out — 1958 was it? I was getting something not just from reading the book, but because of the book I was developing notions about the political debate when it took up content in the arts as its subject.

And then, years later, when *The Twyborn Affair* appeared in 1979, I was picking up this feeling that in certain circles of the landed gentry White was regarded as a class traitor. Possibly the difference between the two judgments being that the leftist objections of the 1950s were based on the perception of the text, and perhaps of the writer's lifestyle, while the class traitor thing arose from White's support for environmental and social issues. It must have been about the time that Patrick White was throwing his weight behind characters like Jack Mundey.

As they say: 'Makes you fink, don't it, but.'

I liked *The Twyborn Affair*. I guess it is my favourite Patrick White novel. But that might be because other ones are further back in my memory. I like it not simply because it depicts the Monaro and its inhabitants the way it does . . . though that in itself is pretty entertaining . . . particularly the bit where Eddie penetrates the manager . . . Was it the ginger hair on the man's arms, the way he cries out . . . is it: '"Oh God! Oh Christ!" Before the final whimper which was also his ravisher's sigh.' Since then around the region I find it hard to keep a straight face when chatting weather talk to outwardly homophobic rural types with their skin of freckles, redness, bristling hair and unborn melanomas.

When Patrick White was writing *The Twyborn Affair* I

was living in a valley which fell towards the Pacific from some of the worst of the hard Monaro country south of Cooma. While I read the second part of *The Twyborn Affair* I had a picture of that land in my mind. And when I went shopping it was up in the town of Bombala where the station hands and rural poor had their ranks disturbed from time to time by one of the landed gentry tribe's women, some Mrs Lushington. Head wrapped in a scarf and, depending on the way the cookie had crumbled, either dressed in plaid skirt and safety pin thigh-clinging moleskins, the hint of horse sweat discolouring the cloth. Watching such characters whole slabs of the text returned.

I read White's earlier books pretty much as they came out, with the exception of course of *Happy Valley* and *The Living and the Dead.* There was hardly anyone I knew who hadn't read them. And yet, thinking back through the 1960s I have this idea that in certain quarters there was considerable resistance to White's prose style. Maybe I'm wrong. And perhaps that was partly to do with the regional nature of Australian literary reputations at the time.

Because of his interest in the work of Australian artists and my connection with that world I heard a great number of stories about Patrick White. That was a period when I was spending too much of my time in the nauseating atmosphere of the commercial art galleries and among their camp followers. Patrick White had purchased a couple of paintings of mine which he subsequently donated to the New South Wales Art Gallery . . . Collecting, it was one of the things he did . . . maybe he still does it . . . collecting and therefore assisting artists to live. I didn't get the impression he was in it for the investment. But rather, like they say, was putting his money where his mouth was. Rare. If I'd liked his writing before he bought that first painting of mine, around 1968 I guess it must have been, I certainly went bananas about it from that moment on. Teaching the dogs to recite whole pages before they got fed, boring people shitless with drunken ramblings about mandalas and/or the sons of Zadok who may come and minister unto the Lord.

That was pretty much where we were up to, Patrick White and me, at the time I wrote a novel which, in 1978, was published by a small press in Melbourne. Patrick White got hold of it, said he liked it and encouraged other people to read the thing. It was only through his intervention that the book avoided sinking like a stone, leaving not even a ripple on the pond.

So, on two separate fronts I'd been assisted by this ideologically unsound writer I defended one dull day in Melbourne so long ago. He'd encouraged me to keep on doing the things I was doing.

He bought another of my paintings about that time, one, interestingly enough, which repeated an image occurring in the first.

And then we met at dinner. This character with the disapproving mouth arriving with his friend, Manoly Lascaris. I got the idea right from the start of the evening that people handled him with kid gloves. And maybe he was sensing this as well. Feeling like a rat in a paper bag, wondering why the limits aren't more defined. The conversation was controlled, it was ideologically sound, it was aimed at him. It was all for him.

Funny thing that, as if there was a tablet somewhere with written on it the things you were allowed to think about, to talk about.

I remember suspecting that there were problems in this. In getting awarded such honours that the world started to tremble before your gaze.

And yet, through that dinner, there were jokes. Albeit careful ones. Kind of 'would Patrick like it' type of jokes. Or his own caustic observations, an edge to them, a sense of pleasure behind the pale eyes. It was an oval table we were eating at, and hanging on one wall a very large picture, made with an air brush, of a nubile girl with her legs open. Some finely wrought detail of the vulva. Patrick White, I was informed, preferred to sit facing away from this image. I guess he reckoned that to gaze at it kept you being born . . . again and again and again. Some kind of hell.

He wrote me a letter . . . I think I still have it somewhere. He sent me a copy of John Cowper Powys's *A Glastonbury Romance* to read. I read it, liked it very much. In fact a few weeks ago I drove past Glastonbury, remembered him sending me the book. Hard not to.

Me and Patrick White.

On the couple of occasions I had dinner at his place he'd cook. We, the guests, would sit in the reception room chatting with Manoly, knocking back the booze. I'd drink Campari because they had it to offer. Then dinner.

I have this image in my mind of a pie with decorated pastry, Patrick White bringing it in, putting it down. A meat and vegetable pie of some kind. He was in an apron.

One of the guests, a vegetarian, made a little pile of the meat on the side of his plate.

Quick conversation, laughter.

I have an idea that afterwards while more serious matters were being discussed over the other side of the room I was encouraging Kerry Walker to suck her toe. Maybe I wasn't. Maybe it wasn't Kerry Walker. Or was it me sucking my toe?

I can't suck my toe, I'm too stiff in the joints . . . from living in this hard tableland climate.

Me and Patrick White had an experience together in Cologne. I went to a gallery there, stuck in the middle of a mall of boutiques, a gallery run by Australians. Their opening exhibition was, of course, a Nolan show. I was with a diplomat. I asked: 'Do you recognise the subject of most of these paintings?'

He answered: 'No.'

'It's Patrick White. And they are not just an attack on him, they are an attack on homosexuality. See over there, the goat with the black circle around its neck and its head, an inept portrait of Patrick White.'

It was funny in a way, a very Australian kind of thing, Nolan attacking Patrick White in a chic gallery in a row of boutiques in Cologne.

I've got to admit that I don't like Nolan's paintings, except some of those predating the Kelly series. And I remember standing there in Cologne thinking of the difference between these two people . . . Patrick White with the sharp tongue and his generosity. Nolan with his . . . for the life of me I couldn't think what it can be that Nolan might be said to possess.

I've got a coat that Patrick White gave me. He said he bought it to wear walking the dogs in Centennial Park, in winter. It's a lambskin coat. He said it made him hot in Sydney. I think of him when I put it on, when I walk out after breakfast over the frozen ground.

Because it keeps me warm.

It's quite a long time now since I saw Patrick White and because I don't have television reception I didn't see him doing his occasional attacks on the vulgarians. But a couple of years ago I did hear him on the radio, talking to students . . . I think it was at La Trobe University. And they were laughing along with his bitter humour, at the tone of his scorn as he ripped up a lot of what deserves to be ripped up in our society.

I thought to myself: *That takes some doing, Patrick.*

HUMPHREY MCQUEEN

I first met Patrick White in 1965. Reduced to £1 9s 6d, he was lying, in an American edition of *Riders in the Chariot*, on a sale table at Finney Isles department store in Brisbane.

So much has changed. Today, we would talk of remainders; the shop has been taken over by David Jones which, in turn, has been absorbed by AdSteam which later bought up Grace Bros; prices are now given in dollars and cents.

Being an intellectual at twenty-two is a risky undertaking. After completing my honours year but still living in Brisbane I was careful to read books that my friends had not. By this method I read John Cowper Powys's *Wolf Solent*. Earlier in 1990, White remarked (during a discussion on whether an Englisher had written a great English novel since 1930) that he had tried to read *Wolf Solent* when a schoolboy but had been too shocked, putting it aside until he was in his twenties when he better appreciated Powys's darkening *non sequiturs*.

To read any Australian novel in the early 1960s posed a different kind of danger. Even though a friend was writing her thesis on White's use of colours, I suspected that no Australian writer could help keep my head above the Brisbane backwater. Three years before Bjelke-Petersen became premier, a squad of Special Branch detectives had parked all day and late into the night outside a conference attended by no more than fifty people who, as if there would have been any doubt, debated 'Is Queensland a Cultural Backwater?' To stay afloat, I had been reading Svevo, Ehrenberg, Calvino, Oblomov and Camus.

The generous US binding on that sale copy of *Riders* encouraged me to sample its first page. White had me at the third sentence: '"She appears an unusual persone," Mrs Colquhoun ventured to hope.' That line has remained in my memory, because of its seesaw of surprise and its promise that White's would not be a normal kind of fiction.

Because it was my first Patrick White, I have never re-read *Riders in the Chariot*. I always recommend it to novice readers as the place to begin. Every couple of years I take up my Penguin copy — that US edition having been exchanged long since for books or cash — and get as far as the third sentence, whereupon I see the colours of Alf Dubbo's paintings, or Himmelfarb's crucifixion, Ruth Goldbold's washing, or else I listen for Miss Hare's communion with the birds. Such partial recollections do less than justice to the complexities of the novel. That its scenes still come back to me as rich and as alive as any event I have experienced is testament to White's conception and prose.

Equally memorable, and of wider significance, was a different recognition that *Riders in the Chariot* brought to me in Brisbane in the mid-1960s. White's vision and prose expelled my concern that to write about this country was in any way limiting. Twenty years later Manning Clark told me that he looked on White as the great liberator whose novels had encouraged him not to count sheep or lashes but to begin his *A History of Australia* as a clash of belief systems.

Over the years I have met readers in whom White's produced a similar setting free. Waiting for the next of his novels kept up the spirits of a housewife during the decades of her bearing and raising four children in Perth's equivalent to Sarsparilla. In the 1980s, an assistant in a Brisbane second-hand shop came to life when I asked for White first editions. He too wanted to write. By reading White, he also dared to hope.

My attachment to *Riders in the Chariot* has not in the least been diminished by acceptance of two lines of criticism. Arthur Phillips chastised White for the 'algebraic symbolism' in that novel:

> But then there comes what would be a climatic moment — the moment when spiritual enlightenment is achieved. Suddenly we are jolted down to the level of the algebraic symbol — that chariot, that tatty Grand Opera stage property. So obvious a devisal can do no more than convey a meaning. It cannot compel us to a sense of our presence in a significant experience.

True enough, but that moment is overwhelmed in my memory by the spiritual enlightenment of the entire novel.

Jack Beasley's point about White's disdain, if not hatred, for working people must be faced. He pictures the factory hands as Himmelfarb's tormentors, an attitude not erased by including the Aboriginal and the washerwoman among the riders in the chariot, or by his later radical political commitments.

So much has changed that today the liberation which White carried to every area of Australian creativity is underestimated. By the 1980s, writers took for granted much that he had had to struggle to achieve. Historians and social commentators, film-makers and poets as well as novelists, fail to appreciate their debt to this achievement. White made it possible for the rest of us to proceed in whichever direction we liked. People who have never read a line of his fiction are the beneficiaries of his breaking down the barriers that determined what it meant to imagine Australia.

The 1989 triumphal production of *The Ham Funeral* underlined that White's expressionism was equally revolutionary in its demands on the Australian stage, though West End conventions have made it harder for critics to acknowledge his achievement as a dramatist.

If he helped us escape from the dictates of a dundreary journalism it was because he fulfilled the commands of the bush school more brilliantly than they had been able to sustain. It is for his evocation of our landscapes that I find myself re-reading his other books when I am overseas. Even *The Aunt's Story* has been an antidote for homesickness.

No one can take White's place because White was there first and gained that ground. During the next century, Australia could produce even greater writers. If such appear, they will have to remake White's heritage as he transformed the family saga into *The Tree of Man.*

Few novelists have matched White's capacity to create a different world of experience within each new novel. Mush as I treasure my recollections of *Riders in the Chariot,* his greatness does not depend on a single work but soars through the galaxy of his inventions.

No one had a keener sense than White that to be a creative artist in our mass marketeering society was to risk becoming a commodity for gossip columnists. What he shunned in life he was not able to escape in death. Those who could not stay the moral, aesthetic or political distance have excused themselves by declaring that he had grown bitter.

When the radio broadcast that he had died, I was breakfasting by Sydney Harbour. The sun and water played their early morning game of dazzling those lucky enough to pay homage at that hour. At the sound of the newsreader's voice, a light went out.

JACK MUNDEY

I first met Patrick White early in 1972 when we both became embroiled in a people's struggle to save Centennial Park.

In that year, Sir Nicholas Shehadie, one of Bob Askin's bold knights and then the Lord Mayor of Sydney, together with other prominent Establishment figures, was strongly campaigning to have this priceless breathing space, Centennial Park, turned into a gigantic sports complex. Their other outrageous plan was to build the complex and bid for the 1988 Olympic Games . . . to celebrate the proud record of 200 years of White Australian settlement, no doubt. There were also plans for a huge car park to house the precious Mercedes-Benz, Volvos, and even lesser polluting machines as well. The first of a number of ridiculous 'Bi' schemes was under way!

In 1972 the Green Ban movement was gathering momentum and considerable controversy raged over Kelly's Bush, the Rocks, Woolloomooloo and Victoria Street development plans. Widespread opposition was building up against the dictatorial manner in which the Askin government was behaving, completely ignoring ordinary people and arrogantly imposing large development projects on people without any avenues for public participation in the planning process. The developers had 'open slather' in Askin's day.

People rose up in anger against the proposed despoliation of Centennial Park. Professor Neil Runcie, the president of the 'Save the Park' committee, contacted me at the Builders' Labourers' Union and came to address the union leadership. Patrick White, the theatrical entrepreneur Harry M.

Miller, the leader of the Labor opposition in New South Wales, Pat Hills, as well as Runcie, all lived in the vicinity of the park and strongly opposed the scheme.

On a sunny June day in 1972 over 5000 people flocked to Centennial Park and held a rally before proceeding to the Sydney Town Hall where a crowded meeting listened to a very diverse group of speakers who opposed the stadium plan. Vincent Serventy the naturalist, Michael Boddy the actor, Kylie Tennant the novelist, Anna Katzman the captain of Sydney Girls' High School (which would have been affected), and Neville Wran, then an obscure member of the New South Wales Upper House, all spoke against the project. To further demonstrate the breadth of the opposition, Cardinal Gilroy sent a telegram of support for our cause. The Green Ban was imposed and Centennial Park was saved.

Community values relating to the urban environment were undergoing a rapid change, and the unique alliance of a trade union with an enlightened ecological understanding (the NSW BLF) linking up with resident action groups and other environmentalists ensured victory for the little people. Patrick and I also spoke at both the rally in the park and at the meeting in the Town Hall. A warm and lasting friendship was born out of the struggle to save Centennial Park — a wonderfully just cause.

With the passage of almost two decades, who would now suggest that Centennial Park be turned into a sports stadium?

Though community values have changed, eternal vigilance is still required to thwart avaricious developers. They are in our midst and possess considerable political clout, influence and patronage on both sides of politics.

I had a feeling of awe in meeting White. Despite my philosophical egalitarian beliefs, his great literary reputation, together with reports that portrayed him as somewhat of a crusty recluse, made me rather apprehensive. Though I had read the *Tree of Man* and *Voss* I did not have then the heightened appreciation I have now of his great contribution to Australian literature as well as his contribution to our 'soul'.

I consider Patrick White's other great quality to be his deep sincerity, and his hostility to humbug and pretentiousness of any sort.

Years later, in the early 1980s, just prior to the commencement of a huge Palm Sunday peace rally, Patrick said quite audibly to all within earshot, including the Premier himself, 'You are a hypocrite.' Neville Wran had recently made a statement in support of uranium mining. I have to admit I flinched just a little. Wran, after all, was one of few Labor premiers ever to march in a peace rally. But the incident is a classic example of White's integrity, because he had supported the endeavours of the early years of the Wran government which had introduced enlightened environmental legislation as well as improvements to the public transport system and support for the arts.

Premier Wran's then friend, Justice James McClelland, was the first Chief Justice of the Land and Environment Court in New South Wales. Jim also became disenchanted as the later Wran years became totally development-oriented. Time out of number the Environment Court was bypassed by special Acts of Parliament.

The Centennial Park victory and the publicity it generated launched a very reluctant Patrick White into greater public prominence. He was to become a great friend of the environment and conservation movements. At a time when environmentalists believed that nature conservation was the most important issue, it was White and others who stressed that the quality of

life in our cities and the need to make cities more
habitable were equally as important as nature
conservation issues were. The world was becoming
more urbanised.

When the developers, the Askin government and
Gallagher forces attacked the New South Wales
Builders' Labourers' Federation and the Green Bans,
White, Professor Chas Birch and Geoff Mosley of the
Australian Conversation Foundation became founding
members of the Friends of the Green Ban movement,
to keep alive the historic trade union–environment
alliance which strengthened the environment
movement and gave hope for more middle-class and
working-class actions, thus involving broader social
strata. Urban environmentalism really had its birth in
those Green Ban struggles in Sydney in the early
1970s.

Though Patrick White remains a reluctant public
performer and to this day exhibits a certain shyness, it
was more evident in the Centennial Park days. Saving
his 'living room', as he eloquently described the lovely
park, has brought joy and satisfaction to countless
thousands of people of all ages. Patrick must feel
gratified, even as he sees 'Nosh' — Leo Schofield —
peddling by on his bicycle to keep fit for his next
gourmet appointment, or Jill, Neville and baby
strolling around the park

A great supporter and friend of the NSW BLF and
of me when the Askin government took contempt of
court proceedings against me, Patrick was there with
moral and financial support.

Before the decade of the 1970s had concluded, the
sacking of the Whitlam government, Citizens for
Democracy and Republicanism, the causes of peace
and anti-nuclear activities, Hiroshima Day, as well as
the Franklin Dam campaign and numerous other
environmental actions had seen White's growing

involvement. Support for our own Aborigines we had dispossessed and opposition to all forms of racism had long been strengths of White's.

This decade also saw White win the Nobel Prize for Literature in 1973 with *The Eye of the Storm*. So, with the publication of *A Fringe of Leaves*, *The Twyborn Affair* and a play *Big Toys*, involvement with issues of social and environmental consciousness did not detract from his literary contribution.

During the 1980s it was impossible for Patrick White to answer all the calls for public speaking. However, his praise for the principled anti-nuclear decision of the New Zealand government, his marching against Sir Peter Abeles' horrid 'monsterail', his exposing the hypocrisy and cynicism of Hawke and particularly of Hawke's fawning relationships with Murdoch, Packer and, in an earlier time, Alan Bond were continuing examples of White's courageous involvements. He also did more than any other Australian to expose the hollowness of the 'Bi', as he sarcastically referred to the 1988 Bicentenary Celebrations.

I have briefly explored some of Patrick White's public performances of the last twenty years, commencing with that Centennial Park baptism. I do this because I believe that, despite Patrick's dislike of being the centre of attention and his reluctance to be seen as 'performing', these contributions have greatly enriched social, ecological and political thinking.

Both in his written and spoken works, Patrick White, while devastating in his attitude to megalomaniacs, to the greedy, and to the vainglory exhibited in high places in our society, at the same time conveyed hope that the 'ordinary' people will usher in a new world — a world in which people and their leaders possess genuine humility and concern for one another, and one in which *Homo sapiens*, instead of adopting an arrogant notion of conquering nature and using nature for man's benefit, will harmonise with other species and with nature.

Patrick made most of us realise how flawed we are; yet he was a real inspiration in encouraging us to fight on. Ecologists, in particular will need all such inspiration in the years ahead.

PHILLIP ADAMS

Despite my passionate commitment to irreligiosity, I'd long yearned to meet Patrick White, whom I was more than ready to worship. He was, after all, Australia's greatest writer and writers were, of course, the highest form of life.

As a consequence of dealing with a succession of them, I'd run out of awe in the presence of prime ministers and I don't think that a meeting with a monarch or an audience with the Pope would have caused much trepidation. Yet to be a guest at a dinner party with Patrick White caused a considerable frisson.

I was, sadly, to be disappointed. White's opening gambit was not merely supercilious but bullying. He peered at me as though through invisible lorgnettes, and in a voice reminiscent of Wilde's Lady Bracknell, said, 'I don't understand a word you write.' After a couple of equally disdainful comments to Nugget Coombs he embarked on a series of world-weary observations about the worthlessness of travel and how he never intended to go anywhere ever again.

Whilst picking at his food he proceeded to pick on a wide variety of friends or ex-friends. The evening became a long, mean-spirited soliloquy. It was a tone that I was to hear years later in *Flaws in the Glass*.

After the dinner I tried to wipe the feet of clay from my hero and pop him back on the pedestal. I'd obviously struck him on a bad night. Whereupon I heard a story about Patrick and Frank Hardy that made me ready to forgive him. Frank has subsequently told me that it's apocryphal, but for anyone knowing the *dramatis personae* it has the ring of truth.

Frank Hardy arrives at a Sydney restaurant. He's a

smidgin tired and emotional and is looking for a friend. Standing in the doorway he peers about and sees, in the far corner, Patrick dining with Manoly. White had recently won the Nobel Prize for Literature which Frank believes is a clerical error. The prize was certainly intended for *his* great body of work. But on seeing Patrick White for the first time (they'd never met), Frank forgets his anger and feels a rush of comradely affection. He will, he decides, go across and introduce himself. He weaves his way unsteadily across the room until he looms over his target. 'Patrick White!' he says, so loudly that it hushes the room. 'Frank Hardy!' And with this triumphant revelation he thrusts out his hand. Whereupon Patrick lays down his cutlery, first the knife and then the fork. He looks at Frank for a moment or two but makes no move to shake his hand. Finally he puckers up and blows Hardy a loud raspberry. (As Sir Thomas Beecham said during a rehearsal of 'Aida', when an elephant defecated in the middle of an aria, 'Terrible stage manners, but what a critic.')

You'll remember that Patrick White was radicalised in the Whitlam years. The patrician joined plebeian politics when a local authority tried to pinch some of Centennial Park. The Labor Party couldn't believe its luck — Patrick took up the rear in Whitlam's panto horse. And when Patrick was awarded Australian of the Year he told the world it should be cut into thirds so that he could share it with an odd couple — Jack Mundey and Barry Humphries.

Patrick was to receive the medal, all of it, at a ceremony in Melbourne and Barry Jones and I were asked to drive to the airport and meet his flight from Sydney. People poured out of the plane but no sign of Patrick. Were we greeting the wrong flight? Had he missed it? Finally we saw him — the last person to leave the plane. And why? The organisers of the event had given the Australian of the Year, Australia's Nobel Prize-winning novelist, a seat in the back of the economy section. Right up the back, near the loos.

Not that this expression of Australian egalitarianism seemed to bother Patrick. But somehow it seemed so crass. Clearly we had to have him upgraded for the return trip but I couldn't get anywhere with TAA's ground staff who had, it seemed, never heard of Patrick White. So I shouted him, on my credit card.

While they were still talking, Patrick White and Harry Miller had a vision splendid of filming *Voss*. In Patrick's contract, there was the right to veto the director. In the beginning Patrick was very excited at the thought of Ken Russell who'd just achieved fame with his television portraits of Delius and Isadora Duncan. But moments later he disgraced himself with *The Devils* and a ludicrously overblown film on Tchaikovsky. So Russell was out. The next contender was Joseph Losey, an American exiled in the United Kingdom by McCarthyism. Losey had a marvellous idea for handling the bizarre romance of Voss with Laura Trevallyn. Instead of opting for the telepathic style of their communion in the novel, he would have Laura go on the expedition with Voss, walking beside him in the heat, cool as a cucumber sandwich, invisible to everyone but him. It seemed an elegant solution to a formal problem, but it was never to be. When Losey arrived in Australia he spent a few days in the desert and decided he was too frail for the effort.

At about this time, Patrick and Harry fell out and Patrick vetoed every suggestion of an alternative director. With the passing of time, I had a chance to produce the film myself and wrote to Patrick seeking his approval on Bruce Beresford.

I told Patrick that I wasn't keen on using the young Australian whom I understood to be his first choice — for while Jim Sharman was a considerable stage director he seemed to lack fluency in film. I'd far prefer Bruce Beresford with whom Patrick had had a long friendship and a sizeable correspondence. (Once, in London, Bruce had told me how he'd burnt 200 letters from Patrick, which I regarded as an act of literary vandalism.) But Patrick would have none of Bruce. Back came a letter that tossed him aside, along with Schepisi and Weir and, surprisingly, Sharman. This was Patrick at his most supercilious and dismissive. One by one he cast everyone into outer darkness, including erstwhile protégés. Later, in an attempt to negotiate a truce, Sidney Nolan purchased the film rights for *Voss*. He told me that he wanted to offer them to Patrick in an act of conciliation, so that they could renew their friendship. But he wasted his time. Patrick would have none of it.

But Patrick's gift for hatred almost exceeded his gift for literature and, it would seem, welled not so much from vanity as self-hatred. He despised so many of us. He behaved obnoxiously. But we still wiped the clay from his feet and propped him back on his pedestal. Perched up there he grumbled away, criticising the view. But at the end of the day we had to keep Patrick enpedestalled, as our official hero. Because if we hadn't had Patrick as a hero, who the hell would we have had?

BARRY JONES

Patrick White, or Mr P. V. M. White as the 'Daily Program' has it, was one of the only three surviving Australian Nobel laureates and the last to live among us. Sir John Eccles, winner of the 1963 award for medicine now lives in Switzerland; Sir John Cornforth, the 1975 chemistry laureate, lives in England. Aleksandr Prokhorov is a special case.

I first met Patrick White in January 1974. He had been named Australian of the Year for 1973 after the award of his Nobel Prize. Somebody from the Australia Day Committee telephoned me. He said, 'We have been told that you are good at handling difficult people and that Patrick White is a very difficult person; would you be prepared to look after him when he flies down from Sydney to Melbourne for the award, pick him up at the airport, entertain him before and after the lunch and put him on his plane?' I was happy to do it and agreed that he had a legendary reputation for being difficult. But, I asked, should not somebody from the committee do it? I was told, 'The problem is that nobody on the committee has read any of his books except *The Shoes of the Fisherman*.' I commented, 'You had better not tell him that.' That *Shoes of the Fisherman* story was a running joke between us until Patrick White's death.

The Australia Day function was a memorable day on which Phillip Adams helped me out. On that day I told Patrick the story that became one of the main elements in *The Twyborn Affair*. He discomfited his Australia Day hosts by saying that he would saw up his award and give the parts to those he regarded as more deserving: Manning Clark, Barry Humphries and Jack

Mundey. He was a complicated mixture of public activist and private recluse. His judgment of people and issues was generally harsh and not invariably sound. As he wrote:

> My pursuit of that razor-blade truth has made me a slasher. Not that I don't love and venerate in several senses — before all, pureness of heart and trustfulness.

He did not attend the Nobel Prize ceremony in Stockholm, partly because his asthma was bad, and sent Sidney Nolan, then his close friend, to represent him. Characteristically, as the Prime Minister (Mr Hawke) has pointed out, he gave away his Nobel money to those who had more need of it. As the leader of the opposition (Dr Hewson) pointed out, he declined Gough Whitlam's invitation to be feted at the House of Representatives.

In June 1975 he became an original recipient of the Companion of the Order of Australia but, like Nugget Coombs, he returned it in 1976. He directed that there should be no funeral and hoped that his death could occur without public notice.

It is too early to attempt a definitive assessment of his literary achievement and this is not the right forum. Nevertheless, the *Age* obituary on 1 October 1990 has it right. It stated that he was, 'our Dickens, our Balzac, our Joyce, our Faulkner', who was 'outside the mainstream of Australian culture at that time', a force for universality and modernity against the prevailing orthodoxies of an 'embarrassing provinciality' and the whiff of social realism. David Malouf, Tom Keneally, Peter Carey and David Williamson owe him a tremendous debt for this.

Patrick White brought Australian writing into the great mainstream of Western culture, but, paradoxically, his writing was full of Australian sounds and images. In 1956 he wrote about the Australian scene that greeted him on his return:

> In all directions stretched the Great Australian emptiness, in which the mind is the least of possessions, in which the rich man is the important man, in which the schoolmaster and the journalist rule what intellectual roost there is, in which beautiful youths and girls stare at life through blind blue eyes — in which the buttocks of cars grow hourly glassier, food means cake and steak, muscles prevail, and the march of material ugliness does not raise a quiver from the average nerves.
>
> Because the void I had to fill was so immense, I wanted to try to suggest . . . every possible aspect of life, through the lives of ordinary men and women. But at the same time I wanted to discover the extraordinary behind the ordinary, the mystery and the poetry which alone could make bearable the lives of such people, and, incidentally, my own life since my return.

Patrick White was a major contributor to changing that scene, filling that void. He was an innovator long ahead of his time. His play *The Ham Funeral* was written in 1947, five years before Samuel Beckett's *Waiting for Godot* and long before Berthold Brecht's works were performed in English. Its successful revival in Sydney in 1989 gave Patrick White great satisfaction and it was seen on television. He wrote of himself:

> Always something of a frustrated painter and a composer manqué, I wanted to give my books the texture of music and sensuousness of paint, to convey what . . . Delacroix and Blake might have seen, what Mahler and Liszt might have heard.

He wrote: 'The mystery of life is not solved by success, which is an end in itself, but in failure in perpetual struggle, in becoming.' He quotes in *The*

Solid Mandala the epigraph: 'There is another world, but it is this one.'

He saw ambivalence in everything, especially himself — 'good and evil, body and spirit, joy and suffering, love and hate, life and death, male and female, dream and actuality, time and eternity', as Joy Hooton put it. He had a deep religious sense and a strong feeling for the numinous.

Four myths about Patrick White should be dispelled: that he was misanthropic, misogynous, humourless and difficult to read. He was not pessimistic about the long term but he had a Swiftian fury about what was happening in the here and now so that the long term could be better.

I said that he was harsh in his judgments, but his impatience was reserved for those who lived only for material values and were preoccupied with the short term, who tolerated cruelty, injustice and prejudice. He was personally generous to many causes, such as Aboriginal education and the arts, including the gift of many paintings to the New South Wales Art Gallery.

He made no secret of his homosexuality but he enjoyed the company of women. Manoly Lascaris aside, the people in his inner circle of friends were nearly all female. He could be bitter and bitchy but he was also extraordinarily funny with a unique gift for satire and mimicry. My last recollection is of his laughter as we talked barely a month ago. I do not know what effect that had on his lungs: his death resulted from chronic failure of the respiratory system.

His themes were often complex, but his style was extraordinarily vivid and lucid. I want to quote two short examples.

> I sometimes wonder how I would have turned out had I been born a so-called normal heterosexual male. If an artist, probably a pompous one, preening myself in

the psychic mirror for being a success, as did the intolerable Goethe, inferior to his self-abnegating disciple Eckermann. My unequivocal male genes would have allowed me to exploit sexuality to the full. As a father I would have been intolerant of my children, who would have hated and despised me, seeing through the great man I wasn't. I would have accepted titles, orders and expected a state funeral in accordance with a deep-seated hypocrisy I had refused to let myself recognise.

At one stage he tries to describe the circumstances leading to his death. He was extraordinarily prophetic. This is White's style at its pellucid best:

Early morning has always been the best time of day. In childhood, gold pouring through the slats as I got up to raid the pantry for crystallised cherries, finish the heel-tapes on the supper table, and settle down to the plays of Shakespeare. Now when I wake, the naked window is washed pale. As I use the eye-drops the first bird-notes are trickling in. Down in the garden, light is a glare. I'm forced to bow my head whether I like it or not: the early mornings of old age are no setting for spiritual pride. Spiderwebs cling like stocking-masks to faces that blunder into them. Dogs point at vanished cats, follow the trail of the night's possums. At the end of her lead the dog bays and threatens to pull me over in a cataract of light, scents, dew. We collect ourselves as far as it is ever possible.

If I were to stage the end I would set it on the upper terrace, not the one moment of any morning, but all that I have ever lived, splintering and coalescing, the washed pane of a false dawn, steamy draperies of Sydney summers, blaring hibiscus trumpets as well as their exhausted phalluses, ground mist tugging at the dry grass of the Centennial steppes, brass bands practising against the heat, horses cantering in circles to an accompaniment of shouted commands, liquid calls of hidden birds, a flirt of finches, skittering of wrens, bulbuls plopping round the stone bath carved by Manoly in the early days at Castle Hill, as though in preparation for the (final) moment of grace.

I repeat my condolences to his companion Manoly Lascaris, himself a poet, the 'central mandala' of Patrick's life who contributed uniquely to his creativity.

Patrick White will not have a tombstone, but he would have approved the words of his fellow Nobel laureate W. B. Yeats:

On limestone quarried near the spot
By his command these words are cut:
　Cast a cold eye
　On life, on death
　Horseman, pass by!

JANET KENNY

When I think of Patrick White, I think of one word: beauty. There is the truth of the unblemished bell in Patrick White's words.

Many people may immediately resort to social anecdotes about personal relationships and divisions. For me, these are the irrelevant ripples on the surface of the pond. I first encountered Patrick White's writing in New Zealand in the early 1960s. I was at that stage of life when all the great historical artistic experiences pass through one like a shower of comets and one is permanently stunned and in awe at the wonder and promise of the world. The harsh landscape of *Voss* was mixed with Tolstoy, Wagner, Beethoven, De Kooning, Indian ragas, Mozart, Turner, Mussorgsky, Da Vinci, Purcell, Dickens, Schoenberg, Bach and Verdi. I was drunk, and Patrick White's cruel brilliant Australia fascinated like an inescapable fate, which in my own case it did in fact turn out to be. So that is what Patrick White remained for me during my subsequent years as a classical singer in Britain. My singing teacher, the great Flora Nielsen, read Patrick White's *The Tree of Man* in a London hospital as she struggled to regain speech and words after a stroke had robbed her of both. I seem to remember that her copy was a gift from the pianist, Gerald Moore.

I was forced to give up singing and I came to live in this land of *Voss*. I also knew from Patrick White that I had come to a land of cruel suburban material-ism. I saw the open country outside Sydney. Without the evocative landscape of Patrick White I would have found Australia an appallingly Spartan and alien place. I knew from him to look for the tiny objects and the great expanses. I somehow had my lens focused in advance for me by Patrick White. I fell in love with Australia with great ease.

I met Patrick White when we both joined the Nuclear Disarmament Party. Although we talked, I was shy and unnatural, and I think he was ill at ease too. It must be hard for an essentially private man weighed down by celebrity to show himself to strangers. He turned up to all the dreadful meetings. He sat there like a man in the dentist's waiting room. His presence reminded us that honour and more, was at stake. Sometimes, as he watched us flounder, I found the silent reproach and expectation unbearable. We were an amateur disorderly mob, united only in our despair about the arms race, but utterly unable to find common ground about anything else. I felt that we had betrayed Patrick White's trust by our idiotic incompetence and failure to achieve any sort of cohesion. Actually we started off well, but as the membership grew and changed, new groups would appear and undo previous advances. I had thought that single-minded passion for nuclear disarmament would carry us over all difficulties. I was wrong. But we were right to try. I believe that Australian politicians campaigning for the 1984 federal elections were forced to talk about Australia's complicity in the arms race with a candour they had always avoided until that time. Three people were principally responsible for this breath of fresh air. Patrick White, Dr Michael Denborough and Peter Garrett.

Patrick White suffered as much as any character of his own creating, during that confusing and humiliating time. But — the bell rang true. We even crossed swords, but the truth of his nature and his great imaginative gifts effected something like a reconciliation or at least, an acceptance of flaws. I enjoyed his wicked sense of the absurd and the ironical, even when it was aimed at me.

I remember that before the launching of the Nuclear Disarmament Party, he telephoned me to read words that he, Patrick White, had written explaining his reasons for opposing nuclear weapons and the complicity of the Australian government in the United States' nuclear war-fighting strategy — words which he was later to deliver at a public meeting in Sydney Town Hall. I was one of the first people to hear them and I was overawed. I could hear ingredients burning onto the surface of a new expensive iron cooking pot in my kitchen. Although I had saved up for two months to buy that pot, I decided to sacrifice it. It took two days to restore the surface of the pot. I think of him every time I use it.

Imagine Australia without the distilled words of Patrick White. It is hard to define the word 'artist'. For me an artist is someone who can synthesise experience and communicate that synthesis. Patrick White, artist, had an ear, an eye, a heart, a mind and a wicked laugh. He also had a verbal fluency which would anyway have placed him the category of great writers — although he told me that he struggled with, and shaped and reshaped his words.

Another thing that I esteem in Patrick White was the devotion and respect he expressed for his companion Manoly Lascaris. He told me that Manoly's role in his creative work was crucial and necessarily under-estimated by strangers.

For me, Australia without Patrick White will be a barren place unless the bell he bequeathed us, sounds in our minds. His vision of an Australia which offers opportunity to all Australians, which refrains from militarism and materialism, is an Australia I can love.

FRANCA ARENA

I had known Patrick White through his books and the media for many years, but I'd never had the pleasure of meeting him. Then, in 1975, with the dismissal of the Whitlam government, many groups were formed to support Gough Whitlam and the Labor Party. It was at one of those groups that I first met Patrick White. I took a liking to him straightaway, but I was very intimidated by him — his strong patrician face and detached manner made it difficult to get close to him. But with time, we became friends. I met his companion, Manoly, and became a good friend of his too. He is of Greek background, a very gentle and cultured gentleman who speaks Italian fluently. Manoly and Patrick are both very fond of Italy and of Italian culture and have travelled throughout Italy.

At the beginning of 1976 I was called by Donald and Myfanwy Horne to be part of a new organisation called 'Citizens for Democracy'. It was to be a group of people, who, enraged by what happened on 11 November 1975, wanted to promote constitutional reform. There were many eminent Australians, such as Manning Clark, Patricia O'Shane, Bruce Petty, Bob Carr, Jack Mundey and others. We organised a big meeting at Sydney Town Hall for 20 September 1976. Patrick White gave his enthusiastic support and came to a couple of the organisational meetings, but had to leave for Greece, from where, on the day of the big event, he sent a telegram which was read by Donald Horne to a crowd of over 3000 people.

> My thoughts are with the citizens for democracy on a night which may prove an important moment in Australian history.

We had been very anxious about the meeting, which was called 'Kerr and the Consequences', as we did not know how people would respond, but it was an outstanding success and the doors of the Sydney Town Hall had to be closed at 7.45, because the place was packed. Hundreds of people outside heard the speeches on the steps of the town hall, through amplifiers.

Speaker after speaker spoke about the alleged powers of the Governor-General, the very existence of a Governor-General, the alleged powers of the senate, the abuse of those alleged powers by the Liberals, the injustices of our voting system and the faults of our constitution, an outdated document which constituted a danger in the hands of those who came prepared to use it as a weapon for their own interests and against what we generally accepted as our democratic way of life.

From the enthusiastic response to that meeting, we were encouraged to organise a big rally for 11 November 1976, which was attended by 10,000 to 15,000 people in the Sydney Town Hall square. Patrick was back from Greece and he was one of the main speakers — we were all thrilled to have him with us. He gave a wonderful speech saying:

> Whatever one's political colour, whatever one's attitude to an event many of us consider arbitrary and cynical, we are surely all agreed that we cannot run the risk of having it happen again. Whether we have a monarchy or a republic is for the moment of secondary importance — though time and the laws of history will probably give us a republic. What we must have with as little delay as possible, is a trustworthy constitution. Without this, doubts will continue to breed and gnaw, encouraging cynicism and hypocrisy throughout our Australian community.

He also moved a formal resolution which was carried unanimously:

> We Australian citizens meeting together for the first anniversary of the dismissal of an elected Australian government, express our continuing concern and outrage at the event of 11 November 1975, and our firm determination to help ensure that such events will never occur again.

Patrick White, son of Australian squattocracy, was an inspiration to us all with his strong views about constitutional reform and republicanism. 'We must be ourselves', was the statement he often used when describing the desirability of becoming a republic. He understood our British and Irish roots, he understood the traditions — but he also understood that we were now a multicultural society, that we had to accept our diversity and that, first and foremost, we had to be ourselves, we had to be 'Australians'.

Citizens for Democracy made him the 'Republican of the Year' in 1981, and he told me it was an honour he cherished greatly. I will not forget the words he told me on the night of his award:

> I want to have the joy of seeing my country becoming a republic, Franca, and I don't have a lot of time left.

When I explain to people that it is time we started debating the republican issue and I get the standard reply, 'It will eventually come, it is not time yet,' I hear the words of Patrick White on that night in my ear and feel some urgency about the matter.

The issue of constitutional reform has been dealt a severe blow by the debacle of the 1988 referenda, but the issue of Australia becoming a republic will become a matter of lively debate in the near future when a group of prominent Australians from all walks of life will be signatory to a declaration calling for the setting up of an Australian republic.

Patrick and I became firm friends, seeing each other often at meetings in support of the same causes, not only constitutional reform and republicanism, but also for the banning of uranium mining, against nuclear weapons, and for disarmament. One of the nicest memories I have of him was his invitation to lunch on the occasion of the visit of an Italian professor. The professor had written a book analysing Patrick's works. He was an urbane, scholarly man, in obvious awe of Patrick. Patrick and Manoly cooked a delicious lunch, and in my honour they prepared *Trenette al Pesto*, a typical dish from my home town of Genoa. *Trenette* are a special type of spaghetti and *Pesto* is a vegetarian sauce made with fresh basil and pine nuts. Both Patrick and Manoly looked so proud when I told them it was the most delicious Pesto I had tasted since I had left Genoa.

Patrick and Manoly had been living together for over thirty years and were very fond of one another. A measure of their love was very apparent when coffee was served. Manoly, who had been in frail health, had been told he should not drink coffee. It was a big sacrifice for him, but made easier by Patrick, who gave up coffee to support him. And Patrick was very, very fond of coffee.

He was a generous and loyal friend, but also suspicious and always afraid that people would take advantage of him. He had in the last few years allowed himself to become somewhat bitter and cynical, a side of his nature I had never known before.

I like to think of him not only as a very talented writer, but as an exceptional human being with the capacity to look to the heart of things, discarding all the trivialities. To me, he has been an inspiration. In a society where money has become so important, Patrick White has represented the 'old-fashioned' values of decency, of loyalty, of being true to oneself — a total rejection of venality. I know his friendship was very important to me, one of the things I valued most.

When I look at my thirty years of life in Australia, when I think of my love for my country, I think that Patrick White, as a person and as a writer, has contributed in no small way to make me love Australia. His talent and his humanity have helped to make me feel proud to belong to this ancient land which gives birth to such fine people.

NEIL RUNCIE

He walked tall with two small dogs on leashes. We first recognised Patrick White in 1969 on one of the regular afternoon walks that he took with his dogs. At almost precisely 4 pm each day, he walked around the semicircle of Martin and Robertson roads. He was an imposing and memorable figure with piercing eyes that fed an ever-observant and fertile mind.

We had recently moved into Martin Road and were just ten doors from Patrick's No. 20. His opening was: did we know that we had golden bough on one of our trees? Patrick had a keen eye and a keen interest in his neighbourhood, his neighbours, their houses and even their gardens.

Testimony to Patrick's interest and perception of his neighbourhood is his 'concerned citizen' input into the City Council's plan for Centennial Park in February 1975. This is some three years after the Moore Park–Centennial Park Olympics fight for 1972 and shows his perceptive and steady interest in local issues.

The Centennial Park neighbourhood came to feature in his works in various ways. It ranged from the apt description of our first born — Sara(h) of the mulberry trees — in *Flaws in the Glass* to the picture of my next-door neighbour's house (No. 4) as the setting for the *Eye of the Storm*, and to some of the location settings of the film version of *The Night the Prowler*. The latter forced many of the locals to become more observant of the nightlife in Centennial Park and to realise how much Patrick knew of what went on around him.

Some of the locals were particularly keen that they did not appear in his work. Patrick was known to be outspoken and often severe in his comments and his comments were also known to be perceptive and penetrating. But Patrick enjoyed conversations with many of his neighbours and was more indulgent than we expected. He enjoyed a good gossip. He was loyal to his friends and those he judged to be working in the public interest. He was a severe critic of his enemies and those he judged not to be working in the public interest. These judgments were applied not just in state and federal politics that fell within his purview, but even in local street politics. He wanted integrity and commitment there too. He did scold not a few neighbours when he considered that they fell short.

Patrick White signed all of the eleven petitions that I circulated in 1969 dealing with some obvious town planning problems in our neighbourhood. Over the next twenty years a good deal of our conversation focused on the threats to our local environment that were the concern of those petitions. But the petitions raised wider issues that were symptomatic of deep urban unrest at the time of the Askin government. Of course, Patrick's environmental interests were broader than the local environment but it was the latter concerns that impinged on his daily life and his beloved Centennial Park.

The Save the Parks Campaign, a coalition of a dozen inner and eastern Sydney resident action groups, invited Patrick White to be its patron in 1972 and he continued in this role, attending many wearying meetings and always wanting to be informed, till close to his death. The campaign is credited with refocusing the attention of successive governments on the need to enhance Moore Park and Centennial Park as parkland and to establish an international sporting and expo complex in a park setting on wastelands close to Sydney's geographic centre at Homebush Bay. Patrick, as patron, must have helped these causes. Patrick lived just long enough to see these ideas become government policy if not a reality.

The Save the Parks Campaign activities had a profound influence on Patrick. The 1972 Olympics complex proposals for Moore Park and Centennial Park were so serious a threat to Sydney's major and most historic urban parkland that we induced Patrick to make his first two public speeches in one day in their defence. In the first, in a skit by my wife, the park's ancestors, Sir Henry Parkes and Lord Carrington, back from the dead, called on current Sydney notables to defend the parks: Patrick White (the man of the pen), Vincent Serventy (the environmentalist), Harry Miller (the entrepreneur), and Jack Mundey (the trade unionist). With his speech shaking in his hands, Patrick valiantly delivered his first political public speech. Then he led a march of nearly 3000 demonstrators which made its way by bus or foot to the Sydney Town Hall. At the town hall, Patrick spoke again, joined by Neville Wran (then leader of the state opposition and later Premier of New South Wales), Jack Mundey, and five Sydney suburban mayors who opposed the Moore Park and Centennial Park complex and who brought forward alternative plans.

The very favourable public reactions to these two Save the Parks Campaign speeches had a profound effect on Patrick. Inhibitions, if not nerves, were suppressed in favour of a crusading zeal to speak out to right wrongs. Patrick was in demand as a public speaker. He was, of course, good at it. His description, on the day of the rally, of Centennial Park as a 'living living-room' encapsulated the needs and aspirations of families in surrounding and sometimes crowded suburbs. His speeches were always written, very carefully crafted; they were delivered despite real agonies of nerves, with strength of conviction and not a little anger. Perhaps he was a little surprised by his oratorical skills.

Just as I and many in the Centennial Park area did, White came to respect the trade unionists, especially Jack Mundey, Bob Pringle and Joe Owens of the New South Wales Builders' Labourers' Federation, who had placed a Green Ban on the construction of the 1972 Olympic complex; Patrick called it 'that concrete ganglion'. He subsequently spoke at a number of public meetings that were called directly to support the Green Bans. I particularly recall his defence of historic terrace housing in Victoria Street, Kings Cross, near where he used to live. The stormy meeting at the Wayside Chapel was constantly disrupted by developers' 'friends' who subsequently shadowed us in a menacing way to our car. The last of Patrick White's environmental speeches that my family attended was in Sydney Square on the then proposed (now tragically real) Sydney Monorail. On that occasion the causes of more than a decade came again to the fore. He spoke in anger but also now in sorrow against urban ugliness, greed and the corruption, that he knew many details of, in high places.

While our exchanges over the 1970s were mainly concerned with environmental matters, in the 1980s they focused on the mediocrity that appeared to have overtaken all aspects of Australian life. He became disillusioned and dismissive of ALP leadership at local, state and federal level even in spite of his initial horror at The Dismissal. Were these changes frustration with the slow pace of reform promised in the 1970s, or a perception of a great source of weakness in contemporary Australian society or, as he said himself, the outpourings of a bitter old man? The answer may be in the cultural and economic depression in Australia that Patrick could well read the signs of and which now is evident at the start of the 1990s.

Patrick listened patiently to my long chains of

reasoning and details of a social scientist about contemporary issues. But he often interrupted or concluded: I never liked him or her. So much of Patrick's analysis turned on character assessment of the players in the events; and I never found his intuition wrong.

Contrary to popular media reports that persisted over the years, the neighbours did not find Patrick a recluse: he was the most reliable resident activist frequently attending crowded meetings. Of course, he did not suffer fools gladly and he did not wish to be exposed to the incessant and inconsiderate invasions of the Sydney media. Patrick was a dedicated and disciplined artist who jealously guarded his time. When we spoke on the phone regularly, it was at 9.00 am by request. The rhythm of the day was important to him. His unlisted telephone number did not make him a recluse. Over recent years the cumulative effects of asthma, cortisone and pneumonia made his limited working time even more precious. His friends respected that and the goals he sought to achieve in ever-diminishing time.

Contrary to popular misconception, Patrick seemed to us to have a deep interest in children. From the time of the birth of our eldest, Sarah, our children enjoyed the most thoughtful of Christmas presents from Patrick and Manoly Lascaris. 'Is Sarah still in her Mozart phase?' was followed by the gift of his own copy of *The Life and Death of Mozart.* Our collective visit to the Sydney Opera production of *Voss* was followed by the gift of a boxed set of the records.

At the local level Patrick was again thoughtfully generous. When local residents could not agree on financing the cost of a newspaper advertisement, for the anti-Olympics rally in Centennial Park, Patrick paid for the whole advertisement, perhaps in part to shame his very affluent neighbours. Again, he contributed about half of the funds raised to oppose the location of the Sydney Football Stadium on the proposed South Paddington Park and Community Centre. Patrick saw this badly located facility (now a permanent town planning fiasco) as a manifestation of the 1970s 'concrete ganglion' mentality, the Australian worship of sport and hedonism, and of greedy disregard of civil town planning.

Patrick White's last resting place was, of course, his 'living living-room'; his ashes were scattered in Centennial Park perhaps among the wheel trees and ibises he made famous in his novels. It is to be hoped that not just the Centennial Park neighbourhood in particular, but somehow, sooner or later, all Australia will benefit from the environmental concerns of a writer who can only be called Australia's conscience.

TELEPHONE: 2 0263
BOX 1591. G.P.O., SYDNEY. N.S.W. 2001

TELEGRAPHIC ADDRESS.
"IBIS" SYDNEY

THE COUNCIL OF THE CITY OF SYDNEY
CITY PLANNING AND BUILDING DEPARTMENT
(TEMPORARILY LOCATED IN QUEEN VICTORIA BUILDING)

TOWN HALL, SYDNEY, N.S.W.

REFERENCE:

COUNCIL OF THE CITY OF SYDNEY

ACTION PLAN 30 - CENTENNIAL PARK

EXHIBITION OF PLANNING PROPOSALS

Name: ...Patrick White,.....................

Address: .....20 Martin Road,...................

...........Centennial Park, 2021.....

Comments: An excellent plan which should go ahead as soon as possible.

I support in particular the proposals for controlling traffic and preventing Centennial Park from becoming a parking ground and speedway. Essential to close Robertson Road at Anzac Parade and the northern end of Lang Road.

More essential than anything else is opposition to the commercial development of the Showground by the RAS, otherwise your own plan will be frustrated. It is ludicrous that an Agricultural Show should continue to be held at the heart of a great metropolis and that the RAS should be encouraged to indulge in commercial ventures in a constricted space. A residential area should not be expected to endure the hellish noise of a speedway or a Luna Park; nor should the streets be allowed to become permanent parking sites.

Patrick White

PAUL COX

I've met Patrick White only once. It was an awkward meeting that led to no further communication. As we parted he suddenly asked me, 'Why do you put little circles above the i's instead of dots like the rest of us?'

He smiled triumphantly. There was nothing I could say and I drove off in a hurry.

Some fifteen years before this I'd managed to work my way through the first fifty pages or so of *The Vivisector* and was just about to give it a miss when I read:

> He loved the feel of a smooth stone, or to take a flower to pieces . . . he loved the pepper tree breaking into light . . . he could do nothing about it though. Not yet. Momma and Pa talked about what was right and honest and the price of things but people looked down at their plates if you said something was beautiful.

From that moment I got deeply involved in *The Vivisector*. It is one of the most extraordinary books of our time. I've read the book several times since then and always found new layers, new dimensions, and discovered new protagonists.

Film has nothing to do with the theatre and little with literature. I've always believed this and still hold that view. However, after discovering *The Vivisector* I thought this to be marvellous material for a feature film, so I wrote to Patrick regarding a possible screen adaptation. I was amazed to get a reply: 'My experience of film-making (eight years, and the film of *Voss* still not taking off) inclines me to avoid anything to do with it in future. Anyway surely films from original scripts are more satisfactory than films from novels.' Of course he was right.

For the next eight years, however, Patrick wrote me the odd cryptic letter: 'Less and less inclined to venture into a film adaption of *The Vivisector*.' Then a friend of mine adapted *The Tree of Man* for radio. Patrick was rather pleased with the result, and was willing to talk about a screen adaptation of *The Tree of Man*. I thought at the time, if I have to get to *The Vivisector* through *The Tree of Man*, I will.

But *The Tree of Man* seemed to me more literal and less mystical than *The Vivisector* and in terms of an adaptation for film less of a challenge. Our meeting was rather restrained and led to no further communication. We were given the go-ahead for *The Tree of Man* but actually nothing happened. There were problems with the production team from the very start. Once again Patrick had been disappointed with film people and I couldn't blame him.

To be part of this tribute to Patrick White now seems a little odd. I'm sure Patrick wouldn't be too impressed with a tribute, and on top of it a contribution from me . . . a film-maker? But we've all grown older, maybe a bit wiser and I can honestly say that my basic love for Australia stems from his vision of this country, from his passionate understanding of this land. Apart from Grant Watson no other writer has ever so mystically penetrated the deeper secrets on this continent.

The explorer in *Voss* describes to the poet the strange spiritual attraction of a country whose centre is a vast desert and whose future he sees as a 'purely metaphysical one'. 'But in this disturbing country, so far as I have become acquainted with it already, it is possible more easily to discard the inessential and to attempt the infinite.' Patrick White's concerns with Australia are metaphysical, made all the more profound and unique by his deep understanding of European civilisation.

In Russia I met a man who, after discovering that I lived in Australia, loudly proclaimed: 'Australia . . . Patrick White, Russia . . . Dostoyevsky!'

Film-making is a lonely business and has few words. During a shoot one searches at night through those dark corridors of silence. In such moments of despair I've often opened one of Patrick White's books at random to find support, to find a friend. I always found a line that provoked, a few words that gave comfort, a few thoughts that offered hope. His vision always brought light.

Like everybody else in this country I owe Patrick White a great debt.

KAY CLAYTON

It has always amused me that I was introduced to the work of the finest Australian writer while residing in Malaysia.

I was living in Malaysia and I was sitting having a drink with another expatriate Australian at a club in Johore. We were flicking through old magazines when my friend came across a review of one of Patrick White's novels in *Life* magazine.

This was a long time ago and some of the details of this story slip my memory. I am not sure which novel was being reviewed. However, my friend became incensed by this review where the critic said something to the effect that here was the first Australian writer who could write more than bush ballads, made some reference to Banjo Paterson and went on to criticise Patrick White's work.

When she had read the review to me I asked, 'Who is Patrick White?' This surprised her but she then began telling me about his work. I expressed interest in reading something by him. Luck was with me because she had bought with her from Australia *Riders in the Chariot*. I went by her house and she lent it to me.

When I reached home and began reading I hadn't got very far when I realised what a great artist had been revealed. I jumped on my bicycle and rode over to her house to express my gratitude for this great gift. Since then I have read everything Patrick White has written. Though there are novels that I like less than others, astonishment and joy are the two emotions that recur with each piece of work.

I love Patrick White's writing because he expresses my inner self, which I find difficult to express, even to myself. For me he addresses questions of class and race in the Australian context and these questions are important to me. He gives a voice to the voiceless people and his love of humanity, warts and all, fills me with great optimism.

PATRICK
WHITE

AND FRIENDS

PHOTOGRAPHS
BY WILLIAM YANG

WILLIAM YANG

In 1978, Jim Sharman was directing Patrick's play *Big Toys* at the Parade Theatre. Brian Thomson designed the set. While he was researching the play Brian discovered a letter that Patrick had written to Santa Claus when he was six years old.

> Lutworth Xmas 1918.
> Dear Father Xmas,
> Will you please bring me a pistol, a mouth organ, a voilin, a butterfly net, Robinson Cruso, History of Australia, some marbles, a little mouse what runs across the room.
> Please do not think me greedy for wanting all these things but I need them all very badly.
>
> Paddy.

Brian bought all the items, put them in a pillowcase and on opening night after the play gave them to Patrick.

Jim had asked me backstage. I'd never met Patrick White before. I'd heard he ate photographers for breakfast. When I first saw him he was opening the parcels. I felt shy but Brian pushed me forward. 'Take that!' he said.

I took Patrick's photo many times since that time, but never had I seen him laugh so spontaneously as he did when he opened that present of the little mouse.

Patrick White in the living room of his home at Centennial Park in June 1987.

In the kitchen, Centennial Park, 1989.

In the living room, Centennial Park, 1989.

Manoly Lascaris and Patrick White in the kitchen, 1987.

Manoly and Patrick on the opening night of *Big Toys*, 1977.

Manoly Lascaris (*left*), Kerry Walker and Patrick White, backstage after the opening of *Twelfth Night*, January 1984.

Stephen Sewell (*left*), Jim Sharman and Patrick White, after *Twelfth Night*, January 1984.

Luciana Arrighi with Patrick White, on the set of *The Night, The Prowler*, 1977.

Neil Armfield with Patrick White, January 1984.

Tyler Coppin (*left*), Patrick White and Kerry Walker pose for a publicity shot for *The Ham Funeral*, 1989.

Patrick White and Tom Uren at a demonstration against
nuclear arms in Sydney, 1983.

The launch of the Paris Theatre Company in 1978, with (*left to right*): Rex Cramphorn, Jim Sharman (*seated*), Arthur Dignam, Kate Fitzpatrick, Julie MacGregor, Robyn Nevin, Dorothy Hewett (*seated*), Patrick White, Jennifer Clare and Neil Redman.

Patrick White at home, 1985.

Patrick and Manoly in their dining room, 1977.

Patrick White in the dining room, June 1987.

(*Above and right*) Patrick and Manoly, with their dog Millie, in the courtyard of their Centennial Park home, 1989.

Patrick White, June 1987.

GLEN TOMASETTI

The saying, 'Books are silent friends' became 'Writers are unmet friends'. A certain author presents me with one side of a dialogue. My engagement in reading and thought is my side. Patrick White is one of those who, as his novels came out, kept me company for about twenty years.

Like any other long relationship, the one with an unmet author is at times harmonious, at others disturbed, at still others, forgotten. It survives and is valued. The author starts the process by offering the writing to an anonymous public.

Through superficially different material, Simone de Beauvoir was my friend in a similar way. Her books and White's are on a shelf behind me. The two people are there as I knew them. I have a permanent love for them.

In the early 1950s, to learn about up-country life in the past, I read Lawson, Furphy, Rudd, Franklin, Richardson, Prichard, the travel notebooks of Alan Marshall and bushmen's letters to him, and many other papers. The message of the folklorists was that the real thing came from unlettered folk or working-class writers. In 1957, I open *The Tree of Man* (1956) and read about a young man clearing the bush for a house. I always remembered the man, the axe and an attentive dog. In less than two pages, I felt it was the best possible account of this pioneering activity.

Soon, I felt *The Aunt's Story* (1948) was the best possible account of a sensitive, intelligent child's growing up in circumstances often alienating. 'The best possible' that I could imagine, was the impression White's writing made upon me. This novel also presented intimacy between a woman and a man through recognition of a bond that leads neither to marriage nor physical sex. This would recur and grow as a motif in novels yet to come. I was still in my late twenties and had a longing for friendship with men.

With both books, my interest lapsed towards the end. Oddly, this had no effect on appreciation of the rest. Much later, when I knew more of madness, I could understand the last part of *The Aunt's Story*.

In 1961, *Riders in the Chariot* came zooming into view with a grand reversal of worldly judgment on what kind of people know about this thing called life. The outsider is quite commonly elevated in fiction and was popular in the 1930s to 1950s. Patrick White brought his outsiders on to a weird but familiar suburban stage and into exotic situations of love and brutality.

Beginning to buy the novels on publication, for a way into *Voss* (1957), I had to try, and wait. Finally, in a London flat in the winter of 1962, I took turns at reading the book aloud. It was marvellous to listen. From hallucinations in thirst and exhaustion, to the look and sound of pure silk taffeta, the prose evoked sensory experience to an extraordinary degree. Full of wonder, I was suspicious of fantasy, yet accepted that, across a wilderness of space, Laura knew what was happening to Voss. White was putting cliffs and canyons back into a flattened country of the mind.

Only in retrospect, I see that this author validated my uncertainties, the apparent separateness of my thinking, my case moth existence as a writer. Though his range extended to other periods and places, he was also furnishing tracts of Australian white society that were bare of contemporary stories through which to identify how we were acted upon and acted.

From *The Solid Mandala* (1966), the character of Arthur and a grubby warmth hung around for a long time. Re-reading the novel in 1988, I found that Waldo assumed a new significance. The change, of course, was in me. Deep into *The Vivisector* (1970), it dawned on me that the novelistic reality of Hurtle Duffield and his sister Rhoda was beginning to replace my own. I nodded to the cold, congealed sausage, the cart of bleeding horsemeat for stray cats, as if to say, 'Yes, that's the way it is, or ought to be.' 'What?' countered vestiges of commonsense. Within a year, I tried the book again and the same thing happened. White was powerful enough and the material relevant enough to be absorbed and to emerge in promptings from *Riders in the Chariot* as well. By 1975, I had written a poem with a last verse that goes:

Herd-instinct still there, I
like Patrick White's Miss Hare;
a dangerous model. Dangerous writers,
supplanting our necessities with their dreams!
'SINGULAR/PLURAL' (POETRY MONASH 4/1978)

I feared empathy with isolated people in broken houses. With *The Eye of the Storm* (1973), wonder that this man knew so much about three round-the-clock nurses equalled my involvement with the prominent theme of a resented parent's death.

A few women protested to me, 'He's a misogynist! How can you stand that?' Apart from two-dimensional cut-outs of some housewives, the treatment of women characters, as of men, varied. I was more conscious of kinships. Out of his life, White went on recreating huge symbolic adventures. The reader was free to have the adventure with or without the symbol, and free to enter, re-imaging for the self, pictures of existence, of rooms, streets, lands, foliage that this intensely visual writer painted.

At last, I was to meet the writer to whom I had thought of sending a fan letter. His media-rumoured personality was withdrawn. I had a novel published and, in 1979, began another. In 1980, Manning and Dymphna Clark came to Melbourne and invited me to bring my daughter to breakfast at the Hotel Windsor on a Saturday morning. Once before, this was great fun. Despondent about the current novel, I went in dragging my feet. The twelve year old was cheerful.

From the doorway of the dining room, I looked across and saw the Clarks with their son, Benedict, and someone else sitting at the table. That's Patrick White, I thought. I sat down, my daughter Sarah between White and me. Rather to my surprise, he seemed to be a hearty man and he entertained. The talk was not of books. Sarah's velvet skirt stuck to the velvet upholstery of her chair. On her best behaviour, she was generally uncomfortable, as I, stuck on my novel, was generally lacklustre. In the famous writer, I noticed quiet solicitude for her and that endeared him to me. He had not forgotten the origins of *The Aunt's Story*.

Before our breakfast ended, I told Patrick White how I bought several copies of his play *Big Toys* (1978), to give away, because it was important. While he and the Clarks talked, I looked at his face in profile, and thought of all those novels he had written and I had read. It came to me very clearly: *If this man, who is hearty, can sit down and write all those books, I can bloody well go home and rewrite the second half of this one!*

I did and in 1981, it was published. Patrick White gave me courage. He could not know that, any more than he knew about my response, and those of thousands of other unmet readers, to his books. For me as a writer, the meeting showed how much one can need contact with other practitioners, especially with those more advanced.

When the novel appeared, I wrote to Patrick White of the part he played in my finishing it. I also thanked him for his novels that befriended me. I put the letter in a copy of my new book to post to him and never did.

To do so seemed a bit like trying to get on side with the great reputation, a bit as if I curried favour in hope of a Patrick White Prize.

The opportunity to say thank you comes, now, in another way. It is a great pleasure to praise and be grateful. As far as I am concerned, Patrick White was a magician and every sorcerer's apprentice learns that casting a fictional spell is hard, sometimes risky, work. Once more, I have just read the first two pages of *The Tree of Man*. They are as fresh as they were over thirty years ago. Today, I can read *The Vivisector* without losing my own reality. Here and there, as one does to a tried and true friend, I can even say, 'Come off it!' whilst continuing to acknowledge the majestic achievement of communication that is Patrick White's writing.

FINOLA MOORHEAD

Patrick White was an incredibly important writer for all Australian writers. Not only because he got international acclaim in winning the Nobel Prize but also because of how he used the English language in relation to the Australian landscape. He tortured it. It is a sincere torture reflecting his own, possibly. I say, 'possibly', for even though his novels express that torture, I would not wish to presume evaluation of his life.

However it needed to be done. It needed to be shown. Just how inadequate English is for poetry — poetic novels included — in this land. One yearns for the words. The words themselves failing, then attack the sentence. Destruct the sentence. And doing so, make sense. A sense Australians can understand.

In Europe, nearly all death is by politics. I mean fear of the untimely death. You can walk to the next place, you can steal the next piece of bread. But in Australia, untimely death for the white man is by landscape. The land repels him, inviting starvation, thirst, madness. Starvation, thirst and madness may well occur in the outer suburban districts. Both Patrick White showed with poetry. Novelistic poetry whereby character became a poetic simile; people reflected deeper truths in which they were mere ants.

Patrick White in some way shaped my view of my world; being white on the great south land of the holy spirit, in the 1950s; being a spiritual exile, constantly asking 'where is home? where do I belong? can I never belong?'; normality stinks. I speak as a teenage girl who read *The Tree of Man, Voss, The Aunt's Story* and *The Solid Mandala* and felt they were great.

I am glad Patrick White was a brave man. He took

on an establishment of literary values when it could not have been easy to do so. He sharpened his chisel and hammered away when many would have preferred he didn't, and in doing so left a legacy any genuine novelist in Australia is grateful for. His white men find it hard to be here. They are not fooling themselves; they confront a reality dreamers don't. My word to Patrick White is thanks.

BARRY DICKINS

I just saw him standing there: The great man and the fruiterer together; the fruiterer with fury bulging from his beautiful blazing black eyes, the piquancy of sweetest rockmelons floating through Taylor Square. I just saw him standing there. A bus ago. It just happened.

The traffic went to sleep for a moment or so. The armies of alcoholics swayed together, and I saw another man who was famous at that time called 'suture-face', whose head was like a football sewn up in a hurry, the crude stitches of some primitive brain operation shone there under the sun that shone over the top of East Sydney Tech; I once saw suture-face consume five dollars' worth of broad beans in a bag in the corner of the Courthouse Hotel; when he chewed the broad beans you could see into his brain.

Oxford Street never looked better to me. I had breakfasted with Dick May, an actor given to spontaneous theatrical utterance at the George Cafe, a favourite spot of ours, partly because it had character and was cheap ('Look at all the roast beef they give you; and the peas!' gargled Dick), and partly because it was simply there. It had no charm but the charm the street people put in it. I remember one man, a street and homeless Greek ex-taxi driver one night tried to steal a hot chook off the rotisserie and electrocuted his arm rather badly; and we followed the outcome of his subsequent court *appearances* with interest; yes, appearances is right as he'd done it before. Chook-pinching and arm-electrocuting; poor chap.

Oxford Street replete with broken men and busted women with aching feet. Phlegm pupils of a slate night school with agony written there. So many sobs it cried

at times like a boarding house. Shuffling and snuffling;
I once saw the strangest sight in all my life in Oxford
Street: it was, or she was once, a lady; a woman appeared to have been in an explosion, as she was pretty
badly scratched and scorched and entirely naked. Like
she'd been blown up. She stood leaning on the bank
blinking and there was soot all over her. These eyes,
light-blue eyes blinking at you as you politely passed
her by. Victim of a holocaust, she looked. Of
Auschwitz. Of Oxford Street, with all its aching feet
and devoured pimps and pornographic children.

The sun shone from the roof of the East Sydney
Courthouse; it seemed to commence from the slates. It
was a funny sort of a day. It rained a bit, the sun got
hot early, you could see the steam evaporate in the
gutter and puff up into invisible clouds containing
pictures of all your friends. It was a romantic day, and
the fruiterer bloke was shrieking about the Labor Party
and Patrick White said the Prime Minister was a cunt.

He then laughed, and although very thin and rather
helpless-looking, he put his arm round the brown and
leathery neck of the short, stout fruiterer and they
argued so hard that spit was all over their faces and
beads of warm perspiration gathered on top of their
car-ashtray-like lips, opening and closing all the time,
at tremendous speed, terribly wound-up and blas-
phemous and insolent and very right about everything
they said: I agreed with nearly all they said, and I just
stood there staring and laughing at him and thinking
what a ratbag he was and how nice and happy he was
and how we should have been friends because I am a
ratbag too. But I was too shy to go up and say Hi.

I loved how shabby he was. He wore old muck. An
old fading ochre scarf that went and got knotted
eighteen novels ago; a woe ago. The white hair, the
stabbing, throbbing brilliant eyes. Talking in Italian
and swearing in Greek. Quoting, reciting, swearing; a

push and shove at one stage.

I loved the tiny street scene; the only ever Australian opera. The street is the hardest thing to write, because although it is very interesting, it happens to be in-human, although of course it is the bootsteps and cries and whispers and bumps and shoves and letters and words and pages and binding and old libraries and books written by him in the sudden sun; the street's the thing.

I recall that he broke a bag of apples over the fruiterer's back: I forget what the philosophical difference was; but it must have been pretty serious.

All the marvellous bright red and green speckled apples bounced down the filthy footpath and attacked drunks in the sunshine of Taylor Square; and the drunks were frightened of the apples. The wild, wise, wide eyes of the great man as he screamed at the fruiterer about what parasites the Labor Party were; how talk is cheap; how they are so middle class they wouldn't know a worker if they fell over one; how there's never been anyone to admire since Gough, and he wasn't honourable anyway.

I hopped on the bus with him in the end, hoping for a conversation, but he read the paper, rolled an eye on me, a great big angry eye, and he smiled for a second, or at least it seemed that he smiled, and then he told me to get stuffed.

MICHAEL WILDING

So: the occasion came to its genteel end. Out in the car park. Finito. Such gentility. Sara has done her best, yelling at the publisher's henchman for pestering her, 'Keep your greasy eyes off me,' she says, 'sexist pig,' she adds, for the military chic she wears, khaki overalls or Viet-Cong black, the knife in the back paratrooper gear, maybe she doesn't want to be photographed, maybe she doesn't mind being photographed but doesn't want to be pestered. She would spray out a haze of pesticide like a cuttlefish if she could. Maybe that hastened the end. Out in the car park.

'I've got some cans in the car,' says Sam.

'He's got some cans in the car,' jeers Sara, 'what else is new?'

Sam has prised open the door and got out a can and his incisors have latched onto and punctured it and he's happy now, hooked into his mother's milk, and access to a box of more of the same, the six-pack security blanket, the two dozen off the pallet carton, 2 doz x 350 ml aluminium bullets, instant relief.

'I'll get in and roll a smoke,' Graham said.

But the car park was all a bit public, arts bureaucrats coming and going, talking of David Hockney.

They decided to drive down to Centennial Park and have a smoke but then they decided that might be a bit unwise, anyway it was probably locked, and then they decided, why didn't they go and park outside the bungalow of the great man of letters, the national treasure, that would be safe, if they parked on the other side of the road, surely if the cops picked them up there it would be the fates, the sport of the muses, the mythic absurdity was surely their insurance. So they rolled a smoke in the protection of the great panjandrum.

'It's like sanctuary,' said Sam.

'Sbetter,' said Graham.

They rolled another one and smoked it too. And one more. Much better.

A figure appeared outside the bungalow. The place seemed to be floodlit. They couldn't remember if it was like that when they pulled up. The figure descended the flights of steps, came to the front fence, stood there.

'It's the car,' said Sam. 'It's a hire car and it's freaking them out, it looks like a police car.'

'No it doesn't,' said Lily, 'it looks like a hire car.'

'Yes, that's what I mean,' said Sam, 'like a hire car.'

It had Queensland plates, the sunshine state, glowing there like a little UFO exuding brief bursts of vapour beneath the great fig trees. Sam hired it to deliver copies of his book round the shops, the back is full of boxes of his new book, it is printed on recycled paper made by monks and bound in wood-free human flesh, pig skin, pork crackling, and the paper has the creamy texture of pigs' fat liquefied ice cream, and the four-colour cover has been celloglazed to bring out the depth, and each poem too, so to hire a car to distribute this already phenomenally expensive production, if Sam can be believed, which generally is in doubt, is hardly to add too much to the already impossible bill, so any computation that the cost of the car hire far exceeds anything he can hope to gross let alone net on selling books, his book, this book, is supremely irrelevant. 'I'll just keep it till they take it back,' he says.

'What's happening, what's he doing?' says Sara.

'I don't know,' says Sam.

'What are you going to do?'

There is the snap and hiss of a beer can being opened.

'I don't know,' he says.

'We can't just sit here,' says Sara.

'I don't know,' says Graham.

'What if they call the police?' Sara shrieks.

'That's a point,' says Sam.

'I thought you said they thought we were the police,' says Lily.

'That's another point,' he agrees.

'Go and speak to him,' says Sara.

'I don't know about that,' says Sam.

'Is it him?' she says.

No, it's not him, the face of a thousand press photographs.

'Who is it?'

'Someone else.'

'Who?'

'Go and ask him,' suggests Sam.

'We can't just sit here,' says Sara.

'I know,' says Sam, 'I'll give him a book.'

'A book,' says Sara. 'Just what he's been waiting for. What an original idea. Why don't you give him a whole box of books?'

'I wonder should I sign it.'

'We'll all sign it,' says Sara.

'No, this is serious,' says Sam. He sifts through his pockets looking for a pen. He hasn't got one.

'How can I sign it without a pen?' he asks.

'Here, use this hairpin and write it in blood,' says Sara.

She prods him with the hairpin.

'Sara,' says Sam.

Prod, prod.

'His skin's so thick you can't draw blood,' she says.

'You've managed,' says Sam.

She keeps prodding him till he gets out of the car.

'Take a book,' she says.

He opens the door to get the keys from the ignition

to open the boot. Sara prods him some more.

'Fuckin' lay off,' says Sam.

'Fuckin' lay off,' says Sara. 'The poet speaks.'

He gets a book and turns towards the white paling fence.

'Isn't anyone coming with me?' he says.

'No,' said Graham.

'Why are you so nervous all of a sudden?' says Sam.

'The anxiety of influence,' says Graham.

'Aren't you coming?' says Sam.

'You're on your own, poet,' says Sara.

'We might frighten him off if we all go,' says Lily.

'Then you'll have to leave your book on the doorstep,' says Sara, 'and the dogs will piss all over it.'

They sat in the car beneath the fig trees and watched Sam bear his gift across the road. The book is handed over. It is looked at, at arm's length. There are nods, bows. Sam ruffles a hand through his hair. He returns. The figure still stands at the white fence, book held in front of him in both hands, like a sporran. Tribute paid.

'Brave boy,' says Sara. 'One less to sell.'

Sam gets back into the car.

Sara prods him.

'Drive,' she said.

CLEMENT SEMMLER

One of the ugliest aspects of contemporary Australian society is the mass veneration of the notorious and wealthy — irrespective of the source of that wealth. Media barons, 'leviathan' bookmakers, developers and speculators, brewers and hardly literate pop stars amass enormous riches which they thereupon squander on racehorses, yachts and harbourside mansions, even though a shameful proportion of Australians live on the poverty line and charitable institutions are starved of funds. Although some of these 'celebrities' are of doubtful probity they are nevertheless sought after and truckled to even by cabinet ministers; and newspapers apparently cannot print enough of their comings and goings and, in some cases, even the seamier details of their private lives. Convicted criminals, drug barons and corrupt politicians and senior policemen are paid large sums for their 'memoirs' and, in some cases, television networks have run dramatised mini-series about them.

Thanks to this mass-communications adulation, probably ninety-nine of any hundred Australians would be familiar with their names and doings; the other one might conceivably have heard of Patrick White. Yet here was an Australian Nobel Prize-winner and certainly one of the half dozen or so greatest writers in Western literature — but in terms of public recognition a prophet almost without honour in his own country. There would be the odd newspaper article about or interview with him when, as he sometimes did, he expressed a sane but controversial opinion about some social or political issue. The rest was pretty well silence.

Ever since I met White, over thirty years ago, I have held it as a privilege to know him, both as a writer and as a man. His brilliant novels, short stories and plays have helped put Australia on the map of world literature; his novels, in particular, were written with a scope, power and technical skill that eclipsed most books by other writers of his generation. And because he reached such an eminence of art and intellect, and was accordingly respected and listened to by those who cared about these things, he never hesitated to speak out fearlessly against the evils and shortcomings of our society: for instance, on the desecration of the environment; the craven adherence of our governments to the nuclear policies of the super-powers; and the political chicanery and corruptness that surfaces too often among our leaders.

Two of his novels are my especial favourites: *The Riders in the Chariot* and *The Vivisector*. The former is an almost unbelievable accomplishment — like some great, encompassing Russian masterpiece it swings a searchlight right across Australia, lighting briefly but pitilessly many of the distasteful manifestations of our society; its crudities and trivia and especially the myopic ugliness of so many of its people. What a magnificent imagination that could envisage the story of Christ in terms of modern Australia: the Messiah as an ageing German–Jewish refugee called Himmelfarb; St Peter as a half-Aboriginal painter, seduced by an Anglican clergyman and become degenerate, syphilitic and tubercular. Judas is Harry Rosetree (born Rosenbaum) who runs the factory, Rosetree's Brighta Bicycle Lamps, where Himmelfarb works and where he is crucified one Easter by his drunken workmates.

I remember someone once comparing White with Sidney Nolan — both devoting themselves to the creation of coherent worlds in the midst of their obsession with the hard, vast emptiness of the

Australian continent. In such an unyielding environment there were surely only two ways of achieving creative work. The artist could either stick doggedly to the known facts of his existence and so remain provincial, like Howells in nineteenth-century America or Jane Austen at the turn of the nineteenth century in England — or else he must populate the country for himself by absorbing it into his imagination and recreating myths for it. So Nolan with his Ned Kelly and Mrs Fraser, his Leda and the Gallipoli paintings — what one might call, I suppose, his version of the *Iliad*. White, similarly, recreated Adam and Eve in *The Tree of Man*, Odysseus in *Voss*, and most superbly of all, Christ in *The Riders in the Chariot*.

As for *The Vivisector* — the story of Hurtle Duffield, the child of a laundress and rag-and-bone man, who is transferred, almost in the football sense (a nice satirical touch) for £500 to a wealthy grazier's family, and becomes a celebrated painter — every aspect of the novel is charged with such violent and Jansenist passion that the words shock in the reading. The intuitive rightness of White's grasp of the artist's business; the way in which Duffield's life is charted from 'the unalterable landscape of childhood' to 'the revelation of light' which his nature, his will and his art as a painter open for him, defy adequate critical appreciation. I had always thought Joyce Cary's Gulley Jimson in the novel *The Horse's Mouth* was the most superb fictional portrayal of an artist, but Jimson compared with Duffield is an ersatz product.

White's talents as a novelist were paradoxical in many ways: melancholy yet excitingly powerful; controlled yet furious; there was a dazzling vision and yet the most exact and precise eye for detail. It is an art prolific with symbolism and images and yet hardly concealing a palpable anxiety, sometimes a loathing for human kind. It is an art the like of which

Australian, even world literature has seldom seen in the past and may well seldom see in the future.

It was my privilege, during my days with the ABC as head of programs and later deputy director-general, to have enjoyed a warm friendship with Patrick and his delightful and cultivated companion, Manoly Lascaris, during the 1960s and early 1970s. I had got to know them through our participation in the informal and most pleasant afternoon literary soirées which our mutual friend, Lady Maie Casey, frequently held at Admiralty House during her husband, Lord Casey's term as Governor-General.

Later I was instrumental in introducing Patrick to a Cambridge post-graduate student, which was to produce fruitful results. During one of my visits to Cambridge in 1969 where my son was then an undergraduate and where I enjoyed the friendship of Muriel Bradbrook, an internationally famed English scholar, then mistress of Girton College and the holder of one of the professorships of English at Cambridge, she told me of one of her post-graduate students who was completing a doctoral thesis on Patrick White, but who, tragically, had contracted an incurable eye disease which would lead to inevitable blindness. He was a New Zealander, Peter Beatson, then in his early twenties. I saw him and promised to help him by getting some material on aspects of White's religious philosophy which, on my return to Australia, Patrick gladly and generously supplied.

Towards the end of that year, though now almost completely blind, Beatson wished to come to Australia to talk to Patrick White to clear up various aspects of his studies to enable him to complete his thesis. With quite wonderful compassion and warm-heartedness, Patrick and Manoly welcomed Beatson as a guest in their Centennial Park home, thus enabling him to complete his thesis.

This was later published as *The Eye in the Mandala: Patrick White: A Vision of Man and God* (1976). It is, I think, although not as well known as it should be, one of the best studies of White's novels yet written — quite astonishing in the depth of its perception. Take this paragraph, for instance, about the relationship of White's characters to their houses — the intimate links to which fall apart as time passes:

> . . . The once intimate link between the house and its occupant falls apart as time passes. The soul, it emerges at the end, has only been 'wearing' the body; it is not completely identified with it. The same is true of the house and its owner. With the exception of Stan Parker, White's major characters have not created their own houses. They live in the houses of others, which they have 'borrowed', bought, inherited or co-opted by right or imagination. They all make a deeper emotional or spiritual commitment to their adopted houses than the 'true' or original owner but in no case can it be said of the house that it is truly theirs. And in the end, the house must split open like a shell to release its occupant into the realm of Being which has already been glimpsed through the cracks in the walls. At the climactic moment in each novel the house is quitted. Elyot Standish and the Young Man leave their Ebury Street womb. Theodora retreats even from her lonely shack, which has now become a trap, and Stan Parker has his last vision in the boundless garden between the ants and the sun. Voss is executed in the most rudimentary symbol of a house, but 'his dreams fled into the air, his blood ran out upon the dry earth'. Mary Hare leaves Xanadu and Himmelfarb's house is burned to the ground. Waldo, the lower soul, dies in the house, but Arthur, the higher soul, does not die the death of the body but flies from the house. Hurtle Duffield brings the sky into his room in his last

painting, while Elizabeth Hunter, who has already withdrawn from almost all of her house and her body, is swirled into the sky in a gust of air. The earthly temple must finally be destroyed, to be replaced by the architecture of Eternity . . .

Beatson concludes his book with what I think is one of the most acute observations ever made about White's writing:

> . . . His work is an attempt to quicken the spiritual faculty in man, a faculty that is so often dismissed, despised or defaced. Beneath the often drab, banal or even ugly surface of Australian society an age-old spiritual drama is being enacted, of which the chief protagonist is the human soul. This drama is being played out in the midst of a predominantly secular world where most people are unaware of the issues involved. White has seized these issues, placed them at the centre of his work and bent all his powers of description, dialogue, psychological insight, satire and symbolism to their expression in his art . . .

When I left the ABC at the end of 1976 and moved to the Southern Highlands in 1977, Patrick wrote to me in May:

> . . . I wonder what on earth you will do at Burradoo. Petrify in boredom, I should think. Every time I go to the country I feel it would be wonderful, then I realise I couldn't stand more than a fortnight. For me the pavement and the crowd. You've got to have something to fight against, otherwise you'll die of bush ballads.
> Yours Patrick
> P.S. The only possible reason I might drop out to some Burradoo is that I could keep a few fowls.

Friendship, as so often happens, grows dimmer with age and distance, but my admiration for Patrick White as a man and a writer never wavered. It still did my heart good when now and then he spoke out publicly (and I know how hard it was for him to do this and that it was only that he felt so passionately about these things that impelled him to the effort): about how he saw Sydney developing during his lifetime from a sunlit village into a present-day parvenu bastard compound of San Francisco and Chicago; about the pretentiousness of fashionable literary awards where there are dinners, lots of booze, television cameras and all the drones of the literary world present; and about the ridiculous Bicentennial celebrations which he rightly believed squandered millions of dollars of tax-payers' money — money which could so much better have been spent helping the underprivileged of this country, including the shamefully treated Aborigines.

Beneath a sometimes forbidding and frosty exterior (which is the true artist's defence against mass stupidity) lay a warm, compassionate and generous soul, with an endearing if sardonic (and who could blame him?) sense of humour as he surveyed the vagaries and aberrations of his fellow human beings. His novels and plays (and I rejoice that his plays have been so successfully presented, for he is a far, far better playwright than he has been given credit for) do not necessarily reflect his true character and emotions, as some undiscerning critics have tried to make out — rather, they are the instruments with which a fastidious and yet wholly sensitive man hoped to turn back the tide of unknowing. It was a Promethean task — but like Prometheus he indeed climbed the heavens and from the chariot of his imagination delivered his magnificent and enduring gifts to our literary heritage.

ELISABETH KIRKBY

I first met Patrick White in 1965, when I arrived here from Malaysia. I was new to Sydney and had spent many years in provincial society. To meet an author of the stature of Patrick White was both unnerving and exhilarating.

I remember sitting through that evening in awed silence feeling totally ill-equipped to join in the conversation, even though I didn't realise I was in the presence of a writer who was about to receive the Nobel Prize for Literature. In any case, the conversation flowed smoothly, dominated by long-standing friends of Patrick White. I was the newcomer and a woman; in 1966, that was an inhibiting factor.

I next met Patrick White in the 1980s. I think it was the Palm Sunday march in 1982. This time, we marched together united in a common cause; protesting against the obscenity of nuclear arms and nuclear war. This time I felt more comfortable, as we were linked now by the burning conviction that the future of the human race depended on the elimination of nuclear weapons.

In the years that followed, I met Patrick White at many protest meetings; fighting again for a common cause. On one occasion we were fighting against the desecration of Sydney streets which was to be caused by the erection of the Monorail. Many thousands of Sydneysiders protested against the Monorail; we were not successful. But then neither is the Monorail. It is not the money-spinner predicted by its proponents.

There have been other protests; for the retention of Aboriginal land rights; to retain Moore Park as a place for people; as 'common' open space.

So when I think of Patrick White, I don't only think of him as an author. I applaud his determination to fight for the causes he believed in even though the protests often fell on deaf ears. When we have marched together espousing unpopular causes, his participation invariably strengthened my resolve. Even when our protests were ignored, I knew I marched in brave company. But, if I were to meet him again as Patrick White, author and Nobel Prize-winner, I think I should be as silent as I was at our first meeting.

His writing fills me with awe. I find his novels and short stories overwhelming in their impact.

It is not just the fact that his novels expose all the frailties of human nature. It is his ability to make his characters so real that their physical presence is overwhelming. They leap out of the page, real enough to touch, to smell; they live with you, they are part of your life. The writing is so disciplined, so controlled yet the emotions it evokes leaves the reader gasping for breath. To read Patrick White is to go body-surfing on waves of words. Even if you can't handle the current of power and passion and are 'dumped'; to ride the wave is an experience never to be forgotten. An experience you want to repeat over and over again.

I have no doubt that future generations will read Patrick White's novels and plays with the same sense of excitement. His contribution to our confused and tormented generation was important not only as a novelist but as a man with a passion for Causes. I hope he will be remembered for both; certainly it is the way I shall remember him.

W. J. HUDSON

I had never met Patrick White and, if we had met, I doubt that conversation would have run smoothly, or at all. It is inconceivable that he could have found a polite response to my confession that for much of the year, every year, my happiness hinges more than anything else on the fate of the Carlton Football Club. Moreover, while *Voss* utterly entranced me as a youth for reasons which I could not explain then, or now, and while *The Tree of Man* gave me a sense of aspects of the Australian experience far more affecting than anything written by scholarly historians of my own kind, the unfortunate fact is that I find his other novels unsympathetic in their characters, style and tone. Never very accepting of stage conventions, I have not much enjoyed his plays. His kind of nationalism, reflecting aversion to mother as much as love of son, is not mine. The issues which have moved him to take to the public platform have not loomed large for me. Yet it remains that whatever confidence I have left in Australian society probably is based more on him than any other.

The reason for this is simply that, not uniquely but more than most, he seems never to have surrendered to group or fashion. He was his own person. And, despite their often pathetic posturing to the contrary, Australians rarely convey a capacity for finding that nice balance between engagement and separateness, between community and self. As I say, White was not unique in this. Paul Hasluck and Kim Beazley senior came immediately to mind in the same context as men of integrity, and it may be more than coincidence that those two came out of the territorial periphery.

Whether such men are likeable and whether one shares many of their views can be another matter; it is their integrity which makes them remarkable, not their manners, morals or views. What makes White stand out even in this kind of company is not so much his scorn for the trashy and the mediocre as his capacity for aloneness, for pursuing his art and his life without protective colouring, without coteries.

For, whatever their idealisation of the Australian as something of a laconic loner, Australians in recent decades have shown a disappointing inability to cope except by association. Artists, churchmen, unionists, politicians, journalists, academics and almost every other kind of identifiable group and sub-group seem happiest when operating as just that, as a group with its collective vocabulary, dress, fashionable preoccupations. Across the board, there has developed a depressing uniformity, with the uneducated taking on a disguising drone and with the educated trying desperately to prove their Australianness by sounding like the most educationally deprived. Even the more assertive eccentrics have shown curiously similar superficial traits in their eccentricity, not least in their appetite for publicity.

It is true that White was more concerned to flay bourgeois vulgarity that the vulgarity of other elements in our society, and more inclined to taunt the ambivalent loyalties of the old immigrant stock than those of more recent immigrants, and such selectivity can irritate. But it remains that White's disgust with the caste from which he sprang did not lead him to seek adoption by other, equally disgusting castes. When one thinks of Patrick White, one does not think of a push. Patrick White was Patrick White, and in that he would have been admirable even if he had not been a man of the highest art and cultivation.

Further, and notwithstanding a degree of misanthropy, he seemed never to have sought quite to turn himself into a recluse. His capacity for scorn was formidable and he guarded his privacy in some senses, but he remained engaged both in that he continued to write novels and plays of a quality only now being matched perhaps by David Malouf (another Australian, from another periphery, able to tread his own path) and in that he was prepared to expose parts of himself in autobiography, in interviews, and in taking up public causes. In those exposures of self, he showed likeable qualities, not least loyalty in affection but, more to the point, he showed a concern for his society whatever the dreadful flaws he saw in it. In the very harshness of his repudiation of what he saw as philistinism he showed an anguish inseparable from concern. He might not have much liked us, but he stayed with us, he addressed us, he paid us the compliment of telling us in his own tones and his own language how we might do better. He did not patronise us by pretending to be at least a bit like the rest of us, and we cannot patronise him by seeing him merely as a sign of contradiction. Nor has his impact really come from his preaching, scarifying as that was at times. He affected us by being Patrick White.

CHRIS WALLACE-CRABBE

Suddenly ravished by procedure,
yellow autumn leaves like
disregarded tongues of fire
are scraping the pre-election macadam.
Life involves maintaining oneself
between the shoulders of contradiction.

Those tufty trees keep on wanting to ask me,
'Is man part of nature?' but
I stumble directed by my dreams and
all the materials of unconsciousness
have been stolen from the dead
by skipping Hermes in his hippy sandals.

Saturated by long black coffees
the opacity of social existence
comes up with little thorns and nodules:
you sit on a committee with some nong
surrounded by an erotic darkness
in whose water you are drowning.

Trees in that blackbird-riddled park
rustling in their bouclé jumpers
do not have the time for emotion
(nor for riddling, I should say)
lazily filling up green perception
from sparrow-fart to fairy-time.

Extrovert wagtails go on writing
God's name in the shallow air,

decimating gnats.
It must have been Wittgenstein who said
curtly that if a lion could speak
We would not understand it.

Leaves, epiphanies and quick birds
may have a gloss of inference
but the words keep blowing through our fingers
down smokeblue highroads of understanding
which others will drive
in their own sweet time.

Peering at a sunlit elm-top,
your gaze irradiated with longing,
do you see its form, a cloud of foliage
or the play of differentiated light?
Like tethered skies these woody perennials
Beguile, badger and baffle us.

Leaves ripple in a shrugged fleece,
light glancing now through the smoke
from heaped couch-grass, lovingly.
Dryly obedient to these declining
seasons, we try to read our time
as a fire delicately burning.

In honour of Patrick White who taught us to nourish things of the spirit.

CAROLYN HAYES-GROVES

The first Patrick White novel I ever read was *The Tree of Man*. It was a set text for an Australian literature unit at the university I was attending as a mature-age student. Mr White was by this time already (finally?) considered the doyen of the Australian literary scene. Thus I approached the novel with caution. By the end of the first chapter I was totally immersed in the story, the language, the other world created here for me.

Having often aspired to the art of writing fiction, I found myself unconsciously copying (or at least attempting to copy) White's style of writing. I was at once intimidated and inspired by his art. I read all of his novels with a voracious appetite and entered with great delight and curiosity the various lives which he so skilfully created with his pen. Each time I came to the final pages of one of his stories I was disappointed there could not be more, so great was my pleasure. Superlatives abounded . . . but at their base was the envy for one who could so effortlessly (it seemed) do with words what I never could.

To say that I identified with any particular characters in White's novels would be false. But so many of them shared with me an inability to articulate our experiences of joy and of suffering. The love White depicts in his stories is often an uneasy kind of love, which seemed more 'true' to me than the depictions of relationships I had often read (and indeed experienced) before. White also was one of the few male writers I have read who is able to portray women in a realistic and sensitive way. His range of both female *and* male characters is vast, yet to me, their common humanity draws them close to people I have known, met, seen.

Several of my friends did not share my enthusiasm for White's work. Others claimed that reading works like *The Vivisector* helped shape their perceptions of their own creative processes. Many of us spent hours discussing why we had such trouble getting beyond the first third of *The Aunt's Story* — though each of us who persevered found great rewards. Sometimes I felt quite formless if unable to thoroughly enjoy or understand many of Mr White's short stories and plays, but always I was aware of the minutiae of life recreated on the page, and thus was able to maintain my respect for his art.

Flaws in the Glass impressed me first with its unremitting honesty, alongside what appeared to be a carefully controlled cynicism. Here was someone I definitely would not like to offend. But by now I was in love, with the enigma if not the person. In my immediate circle of White 'groupies', there was not one amongst us who did not feel overawed by the idea of the man; we joked that if the opportunity ever arose to meet him in the flesh, it would be very difficult not to drop into a curtsy or genuflect. Many years on, I still have the same fear.

Mr White's speeches and essays on political and environmental issues always affected me positively. But why was it up to this by now 'Elder Statesman' to point accusingly at our social conscience (and risk the attendant ridicule)? Could I not myself display the same concern and dignity in my beliefs? Apparently not. We looked and listened and applauded, and did nothing else. But the messages must have trickled through and altered conscience and consciousness.

I cannot explain to a non-reader of Patrick White's works what it is that has made me *such* an avid fan of his. Just as 'You could not put your finger on what there was about Stan', I cannot define what it is about this artist and his works which separates him (for me) from his fellow writers. Sometimes his style seems almost self-conscious, though I don't consider this to be a fault. I hesitate to declare an understanding of his works, beyond what they mean to *me*.

D. H. Lawrence stated that all the pseudo-scientific classifying of literary works and attempts to define them is academic 'twiddle-twaddle'. He argued that a response to writing is valid only in terms of what that writing does to the emotions. Agreeing with Lawrence's view make my task easier. I am not an academic, nor a great interpreter. I enjoy reading for what it does to my soul and my senses. I enjoy Patrick White's work on many levels, but first and foremost, what his writing does reveal to me is his consciousness of his art and his power with words. As a reader, and as an aspiring writer, I feel inspired by what he does.

PETER SKRZYNECKI

AFTER A PORTRAIT BY BRETT WHITELEY

The little signature at the bottom's
so insignificant
it doesn't really matter —
above the pageantry
of luxuriant blues and greens
offset by a writing desk and Bentwood rocker.

A red list itemises
hates and loves
as if a private menu was on display:
SEX, MOTELS, SOCIALITES, PUGS,
UNEXPECTED HONESTY —
reveal quite mortal preoccupations
and a common link
with the rest of humanity.

The hilltop view
opens out upon Centennial Park,
the harbour and Sydney's Opera House —
while a sprinkler on the lawn
betrays the painter himself
as a captive of suburbia.

Composers, authors, titles —
the clichéd influences on a lifetime's work
arrayed without consciousness
or a recourse to vanity.
The photograph of a friend
laughs from a shelf
and fills the room with spontaneous levity.

The eyes are haunted
by their own phantoms
and exist outside the frame of air
as reminders of water or stone —
while the parchment colours of a face create
an appearance of mythic splendour:
revealing the subject
like a character in a novel
                    at a loss to explain
the identity of its author.

GABRIELLE LORD

Patrick White has been a comfort to me a couple of times, without his knowledge. When my novel *Fortress* was selected for the Royal Reading Box on the occasion of the wedding of the Prince of Wales and Lady Diana, I was very displeased. I certainly hadn't been asked. I've never had the slightest interest in the English queen and her progeny, in fact, as an Irish descended Catholic, I have taken a bit of an exception to them in the past.

I was miffed at the high-handed way writers' books were just selected by someone and sent over to them. (I'll bet no royalties were paid to any of the writers.) Anyway, the day the list was published in the *Sydney Morning Herald* I was whingeing to my agent, Tim Curnow, on the phone about this, and his then partner was on the other line to P. White and mentioned my distress to him. 'Tell her not to worry,' the response was relayed from the other phone. 'Tell her they won't read 'em. They can't read.' I felt better immediately.

I used to live out at Castle Hill when I was battling with my first and second (never published) novels, working in the Commonwealth Employment Service at Blacktown and I used to feel so wretchedly isolated and lonely out there. I knew the house that Patrick White had lived in there, and I wondered if he'd felt an outsider. Then I read (in *Flaws in the Glass*) of Patrick White's invitation to the Royal Yacht and how he had put his suit on and walked up the dusty road to the bus stop at Castle Hill and caught the bus to Parramatta and then the train to Circular Quay, then walked to the overseas terminal and up the gangplank . . . It pleased me to think of him on board the yacht for a while with the English party and the warm gin, then walking down the gangplank, back to the train, back to Parramatta and sitting on the Castle Hill bus with the women and their shopping bags and the men and their evening newspapers, just another person coming home like them, except he was coming home from visiting the Queen.

Of all his books, I recall reading *Voss* when I was a young woman and how it somehow blinded me, with its heat and glare and brilliance.

CAROLYN VAN LANGENBERG

I can clearly remember my first experience of reading anything by Patrick White. When I was sixteen, in 1964, I bought myself a copy of *Voss*. Reading it, I learned I was not alone, that there was someone who understood and was able to express in an attainable vocabulary the desolation of the individual.

Until then, my reading of Australian literature was sparse, limited in the main to teachers' choices celebrating the misrepresentation of Australian life as a huge joke in which woman's role was strictly the battling madonna. Sometimes, a glimpse of tarts was to be seen, at the back of pubs or hanging out the washing. The one exception in my reading of Australian literature (until I read *Voss*) was a book I found for myself on a library shelf and it was about an animal — *Man Shy*. All other reading experiences made me angry and I felt lost in my own country because no one seemed to write about it. *Voss* told me I had a companion.

Since then I have read most of his oeuvre. Feminism and living in other countries and under different conditions have broadened my perspective, and contributed to almost feverish reading. My taste has changed, I would hope, from the girl who fell in love with tortured angst-ridden Germanic Romanticism. But Patrick White remains the one who showed the way to understanding that incomprehension is ubiquitous and that goodness is fragile.

FRANCES THOMPSON

Patrick White's books have been responsible for an enormous enrichment of my life. I first read *Happy Valley* when quite young and knew that he was to be followed up. When I got *The Tree of Man* from the library, I had a strange experience — I closed the book quite soon, after a chapter or so, and thought, I can't read this unless it belongs to me, and went out and bought a copy.

Since then I have bought everything. I am quite a bit older than him and moved into a retirement village a few years ago. It was impossible to bring the library; my husband was a great book lover as were my sons, so I could give much away to them. But as I look at my books now, the top shelf of my small bookcase is entirely P.W. I have had very few people to ever talk to about them, but they speak to me very specially.

I had an old Austrian friend who died some years ago — Martha Hirsch — an extremely cultivated woman from whom I learnt much. She was a Jewish refugee who came out before the Second World War. I introduced her to Patrick White's work and she said to me one day: 'Finding him has made Hitler almost worthwhile.'

Later when she read *Riders in the Chariot* she came to me quite disturbed and asked, 'How does this man know it all? He has written what I thought nobody but me and my kind could possibly know and with the understanding of a god.'

My other memory is of a letter I received from him. I was quite young and heard a wonderful Bruckner Symphony at the Town Hall (first time I'd ever heard of Bruckner). Next day in the paper I read a letter from him saying how appallingly they had played. I wrote a cross note to him and said, 'Everybody doesn't have wonderful record collections like you or have heard music in Europe, but it meant so much to me. Also sorry to write a chiding letter as I am one who appreciates your work so much.'

It's tragic that I didn't keep his reply, several pages and so warm and patient. As you will realise I am drawing on my memory but in some respects it's still pretty good. Roughly he said, 'I'm so happy that you loved the Bruckner, but do believe that only love made me want them to play better and I want you to agree with me that we must set our standards high in everything in the Arts.'

I knew then that he was a splendid person to have taken the trouble to write so patiently and fully. I learnt a lot from that letter. I had never met him or spoken to him but he was close to me like a trusted friend. And of course *Flaws in the Glass* and *The Twyborn Affair* made one understand him so much more.

RICHARD MEALE

NICHOLAS POUNDER

I first saw Patrick White on Oxford Street at Taylor Square around the time we opened Exiles Bookshop. He became a familiar figure at the end of each week, pulling along a shopping trolley, always stopping to inspect the fruit and vegetables at Tom and Frank's, the greengrocers next door. He was someone that I had noticed long before I became sure of his identity. A celebrity, but clearly one who did not care to be recognised in the street. He had a look of concentration about him, that I supposed was his own way of being in public and pursuing an ordinary pleasure like buying food. Once sitting across the aisle on a bus I saw the same look at closer range: on one hand it was taking all of the ordinary in, but on the other it was clear that he was someone who preferred to watch without being watched. I felt he would have turned in the other direction had someone pulled him up as the famous author. This was during the 1970s when White had an even greater reputation because of the Nobel Prize and a higher profile still for his outspoken positions on the recent events of federal politics and the environment.

Above the bookshop we had a small gallery showing an eclectic mix of new local painting and photography. At one large group show, I remember the dealer Frank Watters bought a picture. When the exhibition was taken down the piece was wrapped and put in the storeroom. On a Saturday morning a few weeks later Patrick White and his trolley came through the door of the shop. 'I'm here to pick up a painting for Frank Watters,' he said. The storeroom was at the other end of the long narrow shop. Behind the hanging black sheet that served as its door, lay hidden the complete disorder that is the normal condition of any book-seller's backroom. Countless parcels, packages and cartons of books were stacked to the edge of its small space. I frantically began to pull each out but none had the name 'Watters'. I could sense White's impatience down the length of the shop. The chaos of that small room spilt out onto the floor around me and I felt like Chaplin with all the desperate rum-maging and unwrapping. I ran the shop alone on Saturday mornings and it was already beginning to fill with browsers and customers who were needing attention. Fearful and dusty I went back to the counter and told him that I could not find the painting. I was as breathless with anxiety as he was with annoyance. It was not a good first meeting.

It was an embarrassment as well as a lost opportunity, and I suppose it also added to my sense of disappointment that I now believed he had a better reason to find the aubergines and herbs of the fruit shop more captivating than my own carefully arranged displays of new books. I never did see him pause to look at our window. But then it was well known that he was loyal to Robert Gray at New Edition and Norma Chapman at Clay's Bookshop. Serious readers need serious booksellers, and I must have presented a sad spectacle of incompetence on that first occasion.

It was in the 1980s when we next came into contact. I had opened my own shop selling old books at the Kings Cross end of Darlinghurst. It was a Saturday morning and my daughter Louise was earning pocket money with the dull duties of alphabetising and dusting. The telephone rang and eager to escape the menial she dashed to answer it. Minutes passed before she looked up and said in a loud clear voice, 'Patrick White wants to speak to you.' I dreaded to think how it must have sounded to someone I believed to be so shy.

I took the phone and was relieved to hear a friendly voice speaking. He was looking for a reasonably obscure book by the English author, Jeff Nuttall — *King Twist*, the biography of the bawdy music hall entertainer, Frank Randall. Not an old book, but one that had failed on the market, been remaindered, and like so many works of that fate, slipped into the void between the pulping mills and sale tables. I experienced further relief in being able to look up and see a copy on my shelves. It was not a long conversation, and White was pleased to know that he could have the book early the following week. I sent the book and he sent a cheque. I was redeemed. Over the next few years we did regular business. He would ring, usually wanting something that was no longer in print. Sometimes it would be a recent title currently unavailable; or more often it was something long gone in publishing history but which he needed to read again or would like someone else to read. It was pleasant work and I no longer felt terrified by the prospect of failing as a bookseller.

We had a couple of conversations about the work of the New Zealand poet and novelist, Janet Frame. This was before the fame she achieved through her autobiography. We agreed at length about the neglect her work had suffered. How odd, we both thought, that the faith of George Braziller (her American publisher) had provided the present availability of her earlier novels by way of the second-hand trade drawing on the remaindered stocks that had been dumped here during the 1970s.

It was Patrick White who introduced me to the work of the French poet Philippe Jaccottet. His poems had recently been translated and the *Selected Poems* was forthcoming. I sell very little that is new, but was happy to process this order. He wanted five copies to present as gifts, to which I added a further three for my own stock. He rang shortly after receiving his parcel and we discussed the poetry: stark, icy landscapes with fine brilliant colours of emotion.

The most difficult task he set me as a bookseller was to locate a story by the Irish writer, George Moore. It was the tale of a woman who, disguised as a man, worked undetected as a servant in a Dublin hotel. The title of the piece has slipped my mind, but not the difficulty of locating it. I chased it through booksellers in Dublin, Belfast, London, Boston and anywhere there was a chance it might be found. It was supernaturally elusive: Kenny's in Sligo had just sold a collection that contained the piece; a dealer in Boston bet his reputation that we were mistaken — it was by another author, he said. No, he couldn't recall who. Eventually, I found it in a collected edition at the Hurstville Public Library and had it photocopied.

I can remember each of the books I sold to Patrick White, and even those bought by others as presents for him. I once sold Elizabeth Harrower an inscribed copy of Willa Muir's autobiography for a Christmas present. On another occasion a friend visiting White in a nearby hospital took him, on my recommendation, Dino Buzzati's *Restless Nights*. That was not a successful choice.

It was in May of 1989 that I had a call from White asking if I would care to visit his house at Martin Road to buy books. I had always sent White our catalogues, and had not made any secret of the trade in first editions of his work. I never knew what he thought about this, or I should say, he never told me how he felt. But I was sure that he found it all a bit strange that such values should be assigned to books simply because they were first editions. I had sold copies of *The Ploughman* and *Happy Valley*, both of which he would rather not have had circulated. I somehow doubted that he would be selling me copies of his own works, he did however mention that there would be some Conrad and George Moore.

He nominated a date two weeks ahead in the diary, and the fortnight passed with the appointment ticking away in the background. At 11.00 am on the day, I walked through the front gate and up the long path through the garden to the door at the side of the house. It was opened by White and his companion Manoly Lascaris. White seemed quite formal, but Manoly gave me a very broad smile and I was shown into the living room. I was prepared to see a pile of books and for the whole thing to have been over within ten minutes. But instead I was given a chair, and a long conversation began.

White sat opposite and leant forward in his seat. He was stooped and the loss of weight had brought out the bones of his face, but his eyes were brilliant and took in everything. I felt fixed by them and my old terror returned. I was on the edge of my seat, and he looked to be in the same position. The most natural thing to talk about was books. He asked if I had liked a particular novel by Endo, *Scandal*. I remarked that whilst I found its plot attractive I was not all together drawn by Endo's style. It seemed foolish to make such a comment, so I added in a hurry that I was rather impulsive in my choice of books. Not deterred he asked my opinion about several other Japanese novelists, none of which I cared for. (Booksellers tend to develop reflex judgments for occasions like these.) I said that I found Mishima's style to be rather like slipping into someone else's bathwater; he disagreed, but chuckled at the imagery. We approved of Basho and conversation moved to modern Greek poetry and the work of Cavafy and Seferis. He asked what others I had read and I recalled Gatsos, Ritsos and Elytis. He thought little of these poets and extended a grimace lasting throughout each of the names. 'Sikelianos?' he asked. 'Only a little,' I replied trying to summon a title or a line. Fortunately there was no break at that point because he went on to give me the story of how Kazantzakis had masterminded a conspiracy to deprive Sikelianos of the Nobel Prize.

We then talked about bookselling — the second-hand variety. He commented on how different a business it would be for me if I were not in the East Sydney district. I understood the wisdom in his observation. The city had priced us out and the suburbs would see us starve. He asked about England and about where I had spent my childhood. I found it easier to say that I preferred to maintain a sentimental and essentially rural memory of the place. 'School?' he asked. 'Except that a child remains a child longer in England, I don't think I would have enjoyed it here anymore than there,' I replied. He smiled.

Whilst I have always been able to cover myself in some way or another about books, I felt singularly disadvantaged in a house that was so full of paintings. It was impossible to ignore them. The place seemed to vibrate with them. Perhaps in my mind's eye I had wishfully constructed a book-lined interior. Instead it was a gallery. Light was not well distributed but colour and movement came into the rooms from every direction. And it all seemed to come off canvas. He took me through to the room where he wrote. There was a large picture above a table: it featured a pair of huge blowflies in lifelike relief. 'I wrote *A Fringe of Leaves* under that picture there,' he said. I smiled.

'I suppose you'd like to look at these,' he asked. I turned to see a long, low bookcase filled with his own titles. Foreign language editions, all sorts of variants, and most outstandingly, the American publisher's presentation copies — those specially bound up and given to the author. This was tantalising but the dealer in me dared not to raise his head. White is one of the

most collected authors in Australia. In modern fiction
— Australian that is — he does not really have a rival.

It was a rare opportunity to talk over the style and
events of his publications. Dust jackets seemed a
harmless enough topic and so I took advantage of the
opportunity. *Happy Valley*, in the United Kingdom at
least, had a pleasing enough design — well-balanced
black and white typography over sky blue. More
interesting was his second novel, *The Living and the
Dead*. The American edition had, in wide opinion,
been given the best of all designers, McKnight Kauffer.
The jacket for this book is one of the most striking I
have ever seen: a door swung wide open over an azure
field with angled sans serif lettering in banner style. I
scanned the shelves: where was the English *The Living
and the Dead*? It is the scarcest edition of all his novels.
Published by Routledge alongside Beckett's first novel,
Murphy, it had a uniform design around a series-based
house style. Distinctive, with horizontal green stripes
on a light paper, I suppose only Beckett's book would
be rarer, yet I had never seen a dust jacket for the
White, and only a photograph of the one for Beckett.
It was not there and White seemed bemused by my
interest.

I did not ask about *The Ploughman* — his first
regularly published book. White destroyed many
copies of this collection of verse. It was limited to 300
copies and has become scarce over the years. It comes
on to the market from time to time and its price has
risen steadily. However, for the collector of Patrick
White nothing presents a greater challenge than
Thirteen Poems. This slim volume was published by
White's mother when he was still in his teens. The
exact number of copies is unknown. It is thought that
there were no more than twenty-six printed, for
distribution among the family. The author is identified
simply as 'PVMW' [Patrick Victor Martindale White]

and only one copy is known to be in existence. White never allowed a reissue of his first novel *Happy Valley* to appear in English and, as I have said, destroyed many copies of *The Ploughman*. He went to even greater pains to remove *Thirteen Poems* from the record. When the single known copy momentarily vanished from the Rare Books collection and the University of Sydney, White was, by all accounts, delighted. I doubted I would see a copy on these shelves.

Earlier that year I had bought Marshall Best's copy of *The Aunt's Story* and placed it into a collection I am developing. Marshall Best was the right-hand man of Ben Huebsch, White's first serious editor/publisher. (It is worth noting that it was Huebsch who first published James Joyce in the United States. In a rare moment of affection White has recalled Huebsch in a *fetschschrift* published by the Grolier Club in New York). As an author, White has been fortunate to have had several noted artists work on his cover designs. This American edition was an exception in White's publishing history. The jacket design was dreadful: a sickly green with string figures and matching piping as a border. My recollection of this brought no comment from White. It would be hard to better the monochromatic design by Roy de Maistre on the English jacket. The strong personal associations here must have aggravated him, given the appalling originality of the American design.

'It's time to look at the other books,' he said, and led me over to a small table beneath a window overlooking the garden. It was an unpromising stack. Well worn with some of the spines detached and general wear undermining any possible value beyond that of association. There were several volumes by George Moore including the three volumes of autobiography, as well as some books by Conrad. I asked if I might consider the books in my own time and telephone an offer. 'Of course,' he replied. Manoly and the housekeeper appeared and we made our way to the door.

Outside, to my surprise, White took me firmly by the upper arm and said, 'You'll never find one!' 'What?' I replied, intrigued. '*Thirteen Poems*,' he said with careful emphasis. I have always hoped to find another but that moment was not the right one to assess the prevailing odds. His challenge had a final certainty about it. We each shook hands and I made my way back down to the street.

Back at the shop, I opened the first book at the top of the pile. It was a small pocket edition of George Moore's *Confessions of a Young Man*. There, on the fly leaf, in White's youthful hand was his signature, and beneath '91 Ebury Street/London/Christmas, 1935'. His first London address, and only a few doors down from where Moore himself had once lived.

ELIZABETH JOLLEY

Chocolate has its own melancholy . . . The perverse gallery of memory in which the old woman had been shoved to enjoy herself rustled with breathing and paper . . .

Amy Parker is with her husband Stan Parker at a performance of Hamlet. Reading is a rustling 'with breathing and paper' and so is writing;

> He held his head on one side, and wrote slowly, but surely once he began, in the respectable hand he had learned from his mother, who had been a teacher. He was a bit excited at himself, writing these letters, of which the words became transformed — they were grass, and slow cows . . . axes and hammers and wire and things . . . that he liked to remember.

Stan Parker is writing home, from the war, to Amy, like Mrs Durbeyfield's letter to Tess in Hardy's *Tess of the D'Urbervilles*, this is some of the most touching letter writing to appear on the printed page in fiction.

Patrick White's *The Tree of Man* was the second book I read on arrival in Western Australia in 1959 (Judah Waten's *Alien Son* being the first). Since that time I have read and re-read Patrick White. A few years ago I felt I wanted to write to tell him my admiration for his work. Somehow my words did not seem adequate and, in any case, I was afraid of being tiresome to him, so I did not send the letter.

The scenes, the characters, the emotions and the vision created in the rhythm of Mr White's packed and vivid prose send all the feeling for human life, all the detail of anticipation, of hope and of suffering deep into the mind of the reader.

I took *The Tree of Man* when I was travelling overseas in 1983. Someone asked me why I was reading this book while I was in Canada when I had a stack of Canadian authors at my elbow. 'Oh I'm reading them too,' I said. But really, at the time, I had no reply to what seemed an absurd, even an impertinent question. I have thought about this since then and have come easily to understand that I was taking with me a world of people and landscape, a storehouse of experience, observation and compassion to which I could turn. I am not making a comparison here but Thomas Mann's *Buddenbrooks* is another example to explain what I am trying to say.

There is no passive acquiescence and no intensity of the human search left unexplored in Patrick White's books. In reading him, because of his profound vision, I feel closer and more sympathetic towards our human condition.

Patrick White, thought-provoking and entertaining, sets us, speculating, adrift — forcing us to think for ourselves.

TYLER COPPIN

Patrick rang me at home two days after the reviews came out. I was playing the autobiographical role of the Young Man who lives in a London boarding house and is obsessed by words and his desire to become a poet in Neil Armfield's production of Patrick's *The Ham Funeral*. Generally the critics didn't agree with my interpretation of the character. Some said I was 'cold'. I answered the telephone and his unmistakable voice asked me how I was feeling. He said that he'd been rather sick and bothered by the reviews of the production and he hoped I hadn't been affected by them. As the author of the play he said he couldn't be more pleased with the performances of all the actors in it and that the opening night of *The Ham Funeral*, a play which had been rejected by theatre circles around Australia for many years, had been the happiest night of his life. He said, 'Of your performance as the Young Man people have called you cold. Well I think that's wonderful. Because *I'm* cold! You seem to have come to know me well.'

Patrick attended rehearsals every day for the first few weeks arriving well before the tea urn had even been switched on. (I hear he's an early riser.) He talked about his earlier life in London where he wrote *The Ham Funeral* and he patiently answered our questions about the play's sexual themes in regard to his character of the Young Man, grumbling only once or twice when pressed for an elaboration on a question, which to him seemed obvious. For example, '" . . . the young smell of green sap." What exactly do you mean by that, Patrick?' 'SEMEN! SEMEN!' he said. We had fun discussing that one. Everyone added their own two cents' worth as to what most resembled the smell in their opinion and I think 'floor cleaner' was the bottom line. Throughout the season of *The Ham Funeral* Patrick's presence was always felt. Occasionally he'd be in the audience watching the play or often he'd send in a present, card or message to one of us. The cast was never deserted by its author. He was an eager participant when it came to putting on a play. Even if it was at a theatre company which he openly despised. I think that any theatre was a good place to come to know the love and encouragement of Patrick White.

VERONICA BRADY

Settlement in a new place is a complicated business. It may be simple enough in physical terms, especially with the technology to hand today. But settling in imaginatively, that is, spiritually, is not nearly so easy. It involves a kind of remaking of the world. We need not only to find a different order of perception of what we see and how we see it but also to readjust to it our sense of value and purpose.

This may seem all very true but also all very theoretical and therefore not much to the point at issue here. But Patrick White matters for me because he helped me to settle into the world in this deep sense, a world that is Australian, not second-hand European. I still remember my first encounter with his work, I was teaching in high school and on the night before prize day, I was helping the principal set out the prizes, mostly books, when I came upon a copy of *The Tree of Man*. I dipped and then fell into it, took it away with me and sat up with it nearly all night. I did not manage to finish it, of course. But what I read overwhelmed me. Like Dante's Paolo and Francesca, my life was, if not changed, then given a new sense of reality by a book. What it opened up to me was not so much people and places, as a kind of event — a bringing together of the visible and invisible, human beings and the earth, the physical and the spiritual making them into a whole. But it was an event which was not merely self-referential and personal but a matter of presence, of a coming to awareness, which also had public, even political implications since it insisted on community rather than competition, on being rather than having.

Each successive book has enlarged this awareness. Reading then becomes a kind of ritual, of ceremonial taking possession of a newly discovered country which is not so much a place as a state of mind, providing me with a mythic sense which not only deepens but also makes more specific and particular what I already believe.

Religion and faith do not always go together in our society. Nor do faith and the paradoxical delight and anguish in bodily existence which one finds in White's work. What is most compelling in it for me, however, is the way it gambles on the apparently impossible possibility, that not only does God exist but that he-or-she is not what we think he is. The divine is not to be found only in moments of splendour but also in absurdity and incongruity, sometimes even in squalor and often in suffering. Stan Parker sees God in a gob of spittle. Hurtle Duffield meditates on him on the 'dunny' and Ellen Roxburgh meets him, at the end of her human and civilised resources, in the desperation and squalor of cannibalism. There is nothing here of the 'God' we make to our own image, the 'God' of people like Mr Bonner, who is not only a bore but guarantees their boring comfort and security. Here 'terrestrial safety is not assured'. We are swept beyond propriety, beyond good and evil, especially in later works like *Memoirs of Many in One* which brings us back to 'where all the ladders start' in 'the foul rag-and-bone shop of the heart', to play there in the 'glabrous dark' with the possibility of the death of God on the one hand, and of the God of death transfigured to life, on the other.

But if White's God is the mystery of the world he is also the mystery of the word. Few writers of our time have been more ambitious, more daringly irreverent in their encounter with language, stretching and often distorting vocabulary, defying expectations and disrupting syntax, all in the attempt to speak what is really unspeakable, what you do not know but know, to name what he understands to be beyond names and explore reaches of experience about which language of necessity remains silent. But he is also witty and sharply irreverent, a writer with a wicked ear for gossip and for the lively irreverences of everyday talk and an eye for the fraudulent. No one, I think, picks over the 'rag-and-bone shop' with such understanding, passion and style or finds such sharp and lucent things there.

But for all his sense of style, this satiric sense is not a snobbish one. The enemy is dishonesty, false trust in possessions and position and the lack of sympathy and emptiness of heart and dullness of imagination which are its consequences. The disdain for such people is the other side of a sheer delight in people, rich or poor, who live as they speak and act, earthily and truth-fully. A warmth created characters like Ellen Hunter, Alex Gray, Hurtle Duffield, Alma Lusty and incidental characters like the shopkeepers, servants, loungers, delivery boys and eccentrics of all kinds who keep asserting their claims to life throughout his work.

All of this means that Patrick White's world is one of instant discovery, excitement and challenge. But it also means that White is for many a difficult writer; uncomfortable to those who look for the comforts of familiarity but very exciting, life-giving even, for those who like to be challenged and to join in what he, himself calls 'a daily wrestling match with an opponent whose limbs never become material, a struggle from which the sweat and blood are scattered on the pages of everything the serious writer writes' — and, I would add, the serious reader reads. True, it is also an absurd and irreverent, even comic struggle, and this precisely because it is so deadly serious. It is also risky. White has a gambler's imagination. Overturning commonsense, turning the world into language and attempting a style which defies the separation of fact and value, self and world, he walks a fine line between meaning and meaninglessness, chaos and order, risking the fall into personal fantasy, even prejudice. So there are times when his writing seems merely wilful or sentimental, working off in words feelings which neither experience nor situation can sustain. There are other times also when personal dislike or disgust prevail and stereotyping takes over from thought. But anger can also make for passion; White like Xavier Herbert and Hal Porter, is a great master of the ancient and often honourable art of vituperation. Who, for instance, can pillory political or social hypocrisy as he can?

Kierkegaard has always been one of my heroes. Like him, White contests habit, representing inertia as not merely tyrannical but evil. *Riders in the Chariot*, for instance, implies a parallel between the emotional obtuseness and vulgarity of Sarsaparilla, embodied in Mrs Jolley and Mrs Flack and Nazism. In this sense he is perhaps the most profound and comprehensive social critic we have to date. The choice before us as a people is the one dramatised in *Voss* between clinging to the fringes of experience as we cling to the fringe of the continent and making a journey into the interior of the self. He was also one of the first to realise that this journey may well involved coming to terms with Aboriginal people and their culture and with our offences against them.

Voss, for example, associates them very closely with the land, making them the visible presence of the fate it embodies, the claims of physical necessity which Western technological culture in general and the culture of settlement in particular deny. In this way the 'weird melancholy' which Marcus Clarke identified as the dominant note of the Australian landscape, and which he saw as the result of our inability to read the Book of Nature, to decipher what seemed merely 'the scribblings of Nature learning to write', takes on a deeper significance. *A Fringe of Leaves* carries the matter further, challenging the Manichean allegory[1] which divides white from black as good from evil, civilised from savage, to suggest that the Aborigine may be the shadow side of the self, which challenges the whole personality, 'the dark aspects of the self as present and real' (Jung). Until we meet that challenge, the novel implies, we will remain alienated from ourselves, pathetically ignorant and complacent but also destructive to ourselves and others.

This may sound rather general. In fact it is very practical and specific. We talk a great deal about freedom, for instance, but many of us are remarkably unfree, emotionally timid and intellectually hidebound. White is not only vividly aware of this; he offers a way out from it in the 'passion for the possible'. Evident in novels like *A Fringe of Leaves* is the language which confronts us with strangeness and difference, refusing identification with the familiar. But nearly all his fictions are open-ended in their structure pointing beyond commonsense to what cannot be contained in words but must be lived out. Existence here is process, not possession and the 'meaning' of these stories lies ahead of them in the reader's response.

White's work offers us freedom then in the light of hope, hope for this 'something more' which we are to realise by going inwards confronting the fact of our moral responsibility, our contingency and our vulnerability and making out of it all masterful images, as Yeats did:

A mound of refuse or the sweepings of a street,
Old Kettles, old bottles and a broken can,
Old iron, old bones, old rags, that raving slut
Who keeps the till.[2]

As a Christian, someone who rejoices in the paradox of

a God who was crucified by the pious people of his day for what they judged impiety, I find this deeply sympathetic. White defies the unholy alliance between religion and social and emotional habit to break through instead to this ultimately comic, therefore ultimately trustful sense of reality, of a pattern beyond our comprehension, much less our judgments about good and evil. What matters then is courage, the will to be and for being to be in all its ruthless but splendid energy. 'Life doesn't end on the kitchen floor' as one of the last stories, 'Dancing with Both Feet on the Ground' concludes, 'while there is the will to dance'. The way to cure the paralysis of will, hardness of heart and dullness of sympathy which affect so many of us, especially the virtuous, lies here, not in the heroic attempt to create value within ourselves but to join in the dance.

So White's imaginative virtuosity and insouciance are not just aesthetic matters. Flamboyance becomes a form of prayer, of letting go and letting be, paying tribute to the 'privilege and panic of mortality' to what is the 'hypocrisy and cynicism, hunger and despair'. I like to think of him, then, as Yeats's 'Malachi Stilt-Jack' affirming life in the face of death:

I through the terrible novelty of light, stalk on,
stalk on;
Those great sea-horses bear their teeth and
laugh at the dawn.[3]

NOTES

(1) Abdul JanMohamed, 'The economy of Manichean Allegory: The function of Racial Difference in Colonization and Literature' in Henry Louis Gates (ed), *Race, Writing and Difference* London: University of Chicago Press, 1986.

(2) W. B. Yeats, 'Circus Animals' Desertion' in the *Collected Poems of W. B. Yeats* (London: Macmillan), 1971, pp 391-392.

(3) W. B. Yeats, 'High Talk' in the *Collected Poems of W. B. Yeats* (London: Macmillan), 1971, pp 385–6.

RAY WILLBANK

On 24 January, 1988, six months after I had had tea with Patrick White at his home in Sydney I was delighted to see him sparring in a ten-second interview on American television. Both *Good Morning America* and the *ABC Nightly News* showed the re-enactment of the arrival of the First Fleet at Sydney Harbour along with protesting Aborigines, fireworks, and an appearance by Prince Charles and Princess Diana. The report switched from a laughing Prince and Princess to Patrick White sitting in apparent ease and good health in his garden. Asked what he thought of the Bicentennial celebration, White, in the softest of voices said, 'Well, I think it's shocking the way the royal goons are going to be here most of the year.' He added, 'I can't really see an awful lot to be proud about in our past, and certainly not in our present.'

Six months earlier he had told me the same thing, citing the transportation of convicts, the treatment of the Aborigines, and the allegiance to monarchy as Australian blemishes. In a letter he had written to me, he said, 'I am too ashamed of so much that has gone on in our history and can't accept the pouring of millions into a "festival" when we do so little for the Aboriginals and the many contemporary white Australians who are starving. The Queen of England will be coming to open the new and unnecessarily extravagant Parliament House and her spawn will be popping up all over the country at various moments.' He intended to protest in his own way, he said. He would refuse to allow any play of his to be staged during the Bicentennial year or any work of his to be published. True to his word, when it appeared that the publication date of his new book *Three Uneasy Pieces* was going to be delayed until 1988, he took it from one Melbourne publisher and gave it to another who would bring it out in 1987.

Patrick White as I saw him at seventy-five, was a man of strong convictions with no timidity of expression. As we talked in July of 1987 I found him angry and impatient with his fellow Australians. Though arthritic and asthmatic and needing his rest, he was not, happily, as he had pictured himself a few months earlier in his letter to me. 'I am crumbling,' he had written, 'osteoporosis, a filling chest, glaucoma and a hernia.' He had invited me to visit him, lamenting doubtfully, 'if I am still around'. From his letter, I had expected to find him, if still around, decrepit and depressed. Instead of gasping his last, I found him scrappy and vituperative. The hernia had been repaired, the chest was clear, and he wasn't dependent upon the cane he carried.

When I arrived at the white frame house on Martin Road on the sunny, chilly July morning, White's longtime companion Manoly Lascaris, in sweater and gloves, was working in the front garden among azaleas, camellias and a few stalky red impatiens. Their Italian gardener had quit some months before, Manoly explained to me, and he was tending the flowers. Crippled for a while by arthritis, Manoly had undergone six months of acupuncture and now he was able to move without pain and to enjoy the garden.

Manoly took me around to a side entrance to the house. Patrick White must have been watching from behind the curtain — he must have been — for he opened the door as soon as we were on the steps. And there he was — a big man, white hair, deep-set eyes, drawing me into the house with a handshake and a point of his cane. He led me through a short hall into the living room and seated himself across from me, positioning himself with a direct beam of bright light shining on his eyes. I remembered the glaucoma. As a playful put down or a blunt truth, I never knew which, he said, 'I've forgotten your name. Is it Millikin or Millbank, or something like that?' Thus began two hours of conversation, gossipy, bitchy, full of laughter and complaints and pronouncements, a roller-coaster ride that touched on everything but his work. Any attempt on my part in that direction was masterfully diverted, as I had expected it would be.

In *Flaws in the Glass* White spoke of visitors who came expecting him to be like one of the characters in his novels, or to be full of high sentence and philosophical pronouncements. They got a surprise, he said. And yet despite what he said, the depth and the presence were there. And even with all the laughter and kindness, I knew I was with the great man and was never comfortable enough to forget it.

Impatient under the bright light (too strong? not strong enough?), White soon led Manoly and me down the hall toward the kitchen where he proposed to make tea and take it outside. I glanced about, wanting to linger in front of walls covered with startling paintings, to inspect bold colours thick on canvas. I wanted to examine a long case filled with White's own books published in various English and foreign language editions. I paused at a utility staircase leading to the second floor, thinking that it was nothing like the one in *Eye of the Storm*, an elaborate affair that Sister de Santis had moved ponderously up and down as she waited on Elizabeth Hunter. I had thought White had used his home as a setting in *Eye*, but I could see nothing in it that I recognised from the novel. Obviously, I was wrong.

In the kitchen Patrick got the tea things together, heated water in a blue coffee pot, put brown mugs and saucers on a tray, took a box of cookies from a plastic container on a shelf. 'You don't mind if I put the box on the tray, if I leave them in the box, do you?' he asked.

I carried the tray to the back door, where Patrick angrily shouted down two little dogs, one white, one orange. I asked about cats. I'd seen cats in pictures with him. 'We've always had cats,' he said. 'But now we're without one. Cats usually live a long time. We're too old,' he said, sadly, 'to start a new one.'

We crossed a narrow lawn to a raised deck covered by a twiggy canopy, leafless now in the winter. Manoly warned us to wait before sitting down. 'Bird shit,' he said, cleaning off the chairs.

The house and yard are on ground higher than the street. Beyond Patrick, in the distance through the trees, I could see commercial buildings. It wouldn't be long, Patrick complained, until all the houses along his leafy green street would be torn down for 'progress'. 'It is sad,' he had written me, 'that such a beautiful world can also be so vile.'

Over tea we spoke of Tasmania where I had just been. 'We were there once,' Patrick said, 'to escape the Nobel Prize. It's a lonely place, isn't it? I could still hear the rattle of the convict chains. I was there once before, when I was ten years old. I could have heard the chains even better then, if I had known what I was hearing.'

He spoke of Tasmanian farmer-poet Barney Roberts who had been captured during the Second World War and how much he liked his poetry. He spoke of New Zealander Janet Frame and his regard for her fiction, and told warm, comical stories of his friend Thea Astley who had once been his neighbour when she and her family were living at Epping, a short distance from his home at Castle Hill. He remembered the time he had invited the American actress Alexis Smith to meet Thea, thinking she might want to star in a movie of

Thea's novel *A Descant for Gossips*. 'We all got along,' he said, 'but nothing ever came of the movie idea.'

Had he seen David Malouf's new play, *Blood Relations*, which was then on stage in Sydney? I asked. He had, he answered. 'Did you like it?' I persisted. He looked through me. 'I like David,' he said.

I tried to remember other questions on my list. 'You met Frieda Lawrence once when you were in New Mexico. What was she like?'

He didn't pause. 'Jolly,' he said. 'Not at all the earth mother you'd expect.' His tone told me the subject did not interest him.

So I shifted again. White was wearing a grey crew neck sweater. From his neck hung an ivory-coloured ink pen. On another cord hung a fat, misshapen cross. I asked him about the cross, what it meant that he was wearing it.

He smiled, as if in anticipation of his answer. 'This was given to me by a nun who lives in a tree. She makes these crosses. And what I wonder is,' he grinned mischievously, 'if she keeps making these crosses, what's going to happen to her home?' We laughed. Manoly poured more tea.

I remembered that I had a small present for Patrick in my bag. Before I had left the States I had cast about for something to give him. I love his work and I was grateful that he had agreed to see me. So I wanted to hand him something, though I doubted if I could please him. I had found stuck away in a desk in my home in Memphis a small, black wool, satin-lined Greek coin purse that I had bought on a whim some years before. It was a small piece, not as big as my hand, but fitted with a long black cord, if one wanted to wear it. Embroidered in white on the black wool was the outline of a wise man, Confucius perhaps, sitting on a bench. Behind him, around him, were tiny purple flowers, pinheads of colour. Purple, the colour of transcendence. Back at home, it had seemed the perfect gift for him. Now, as I removed it from my bag and handed it to him, I wondered if I was being silly. 'I don't know why I want to give this to you,' I said. 'But the purple spots remind me of the purple you use so often in your novels. Particularly *The Twyborn Affair*.'

'Do I?' he said. And that was all he said.

He looked at it a moment, then promptly put it around his neck, layering it with the pen and the wooden cross. In wondered if some day hence he would have an American story to go with that of the nun. 'Some people tell me,' he said, his eyes on me, 'this cross looks like a piece of sucked gingerbread'. His eyes widened and we burst out laughing.

Flickers of shade dappled the sun on Patrick White's face as we sat under the naked branches of the arbour, our conversation bumping into silences as it wound down. I'd been mesmerised by the eyes, hard and hostile as he raved about the growth of Sydney or the stupidity of the Bicentennial, distant when I bored him, warm and laughing when he touched on something that he enjoyed. There was also pain and nastiness and impatience. I kept thinking of Milton's Satan, who had been to the heights and depths and seen it all, of Lazarus, who had come back to tell all. White was wrong if he thought that a visitor who came seeking the author found only the man. The eyes belonged to both.

I asked him if I could take his picture. He got up and stood in the sunlight in front of a shrub and said with a kind of sadness, 'How many, many times I've stood in this spot and had my picture made.' I focused longer than I had to, not wanting to give up those eyes.

Back in the kitchen, White got out the Yellow Pages and looked up the telephone number of the Cosmopolitan Coffee Shop where I was to meet a friend. He insisted on dialling the number. When the arrangements were made, Manoly got out the Fiat and drove me around Centennial Park to the coffee shop. Along the way we talked of Manoly's American mother who had recently died in Vermont in her nineties and of his forty-five year relationship with Patrick White. He double-parked in front of the Cosmopolitan and continued to tell me stories about Patrick in a gentle and loving voice until impatient traffic forced me from the Fiat and him along his way.

I would love to tell what he said, this other half of the Living Legend. But even now I can hear Patrick White's words in one of his moments of bitterness as we talked. 'You'll probably go out and tell X (famous writer) just what I said about her. Everybody tells everything.'

Well, I haven't told all. And with Patrick White strong enough to shout down the monarchy on round-the-world television I wouldn't dare tell it all, even if I wanted to.

ELIZABETH RIDDELL

HIS DAY

That morning he felt not too old
to go to the double windows and watch the birds.

Later he telephoned to report
a spotted pardalote impetuously had left the nest
and spiralled down, drifting on indifferent air
discovering flight too soon

to fall bewildered in the small shade of windflowers
while above the community chattered,
before it levitated back laboriously
from branch to branch
into the nest. Then all quietened.

Last week he had read in a magazine that in Costa Rica
they do not kill the birds.
Instead, they kill the people, he observed.

That afternoon he sat at a table on the flagstones
and drank tea. Manoly walked the dogs
around pine thickets in the drowsy park.
A friend came. He signed a book with the bold flowing
    name.
The terrier shifted on its haunches,
scratched, muttered and appealed.

He wore a sweater of a certain dashing green
and a fisherman's woollen tasselled cap
a traveller had brought him from Cascais.
He gave the terrier a biscuit

and when the sun paused behind a calligraphy of leaves
he read its message and rose and walked inside.
And as he walked a great wracking cough
risen from the humid pastures and lake shore of his
      youth
seized him and shook him in its jaws.

The day was almost over. In the glimmer of mahogany
and the profound presence of enormous paintings
the light was gradually dimmed and then went out.
The man lay straitly in his bed.

Below him on the floor the terrier twitched and snored.

Andrew Riemer

The only time I met Patrick White was at an academic dinner party in the mid-60s. The conversation was desultory, even banal — the Greek Islands, the danger of contracting mumps as an adult (one of the invited guests had gone down the previous day with a particularly bad dose), a few scraps of academic gossip. Yet the evening had an unforgettable intensity. Not because of meeting a famous writer, but as a result of the electricity — felt even by those around the table who knew him well — generated by a curious mixture of diffidence and barely disguised hostility that flowed out of him. White was suspicious, as he was entitled to be, fearful, no doubt, of getting too close to the hated tribe of academic scribes at whose hands, he felt, he had suffered so much.

That intensity may not have been characteristic of the man, but it is undoubtedly characteristic of his work. It is impossible to be indifferent to Patrick White. It is not possible to remain unmoved by his vision, even if that vision should prove unpalatable, possibly disgusting. His commitment to his idiosyncratic view of the world remained constant throughout a career that saw the emergence of Australian literature from being a quaint backwater of the British literary empire to something that the rest of the world had to acknowledge, no matter how grudgingly.

Yet as our literature grew and prospered to a degree, and as it came to be embraced by that somewhat sinister phenomenon known as 'Austlit', White's stocks began to fall from the late 1970s onwards. He did not speak with the voice of contemporary Australia, at least as the custodians of literature heard it. His social and

political pronouncements — delivered in those
unmistakably prophetic and sepulchral tones — may
have appealed to an increasingly large section of the
population. He even managed to find something he
had sought throughout his career: an audience for his
plays. His reading public probably remained as large
(or as small) as it had always been. But younger
writers, and many sections of the literary establishment, began to turn their backs on him. His work
came increasingly to represent something that
Australian writers felt they had to discard — an elitism,
a dedication to high culture and, worst of all in the
demonology of contemporary literary thought,
decidedly Eurocentric tendencies. Go to any conference on Austlit these days, you won't find many papers
on Patrick White.

All writers must suffer the vicissitudes of fashion. I
suspect that for a couple of decades White's reputation
will decline. His books will probably begin to disappear
from school syllabuses and university reading lists. The
day may come when some of his novels will go out of
print temporarily. It is even possible that his last substantial work of fiction, that largely unsatisfactory essay
in Postmodernism *The Memoirs of Many in One*, will be
the novel to speak most eloquently to future readers.

Nevertheless, once the dust has settled, when the
squabbles and rivalries of the day will have become as
quaint and curious as the famous disputes of the past,
White will have his day. For undoubtedly he was a very
great writer, the greatest Australian novelist of the
century — and I say this even though there is a decade
of it left — and a writer, moreover, capable of speaking
to people beyond his immediate society, culture and
time.

White's cosmopolitan sensibility, which looked
towards the old world while locating its interests and
passions in the newest of the new, is the characteristic

that will ensure him a place among the literary greats. For he was, in a thoroughly honourable and fully justified sense, an heir of the great novelists of the past. The intensity of vision which I glimpsed briefly at a humdrum dinner party nearly three decades ago saw the world as Dostoevsky, as Tolstoy and as Thomas Mann saw it. Like them, White was tormented by the paradox of humanity. Like them, he recognised the terrible ambiguity at the heart of each man and woman. From the tentative beginnings of *Happy Valley* and *The Living and the Dead* to the triumphant black comedy of *The Twyborn Affair*, his gaze rarely faltered. The novels, and one or two of the plays, are filled with characters capable of exploring the depths of suffering, even of depravity, while ascending to visionary heights. The lonely visionary, the outcast, the human being who dwells at the edge of society, or indeed beyond it, continued to fascinate and to disturb him throughout his career. Eddie Twyborn, achieving illumination as he is blown to smithereens in the London Blitz, looks back towards Elizabeth Hunter in *The Eye of the Storm* as she throws off her corrupt social face in the face of the great cyclone on Brumby Island, or to Stan Parker in *The Tree of Man* discovering God in a gob of spittle while surrounded by a mandala of cabbages.

Like the great writers of the last century, with whom he may properly be compared, even if his achievement should prove to be lesser than theirs, White spoke with many voices. What has been difficult for some to recognise is that strain of mordant comedy that accompanies many of his metaphysical peaks, enriching rather than diminishing the intensity of those moments. When Arthur Brown's concentration on the mystery of things in *The Solid Mandala* is momentarily diverted by a farting dog, the indecent and the indecorum somehow allows us to accept the validity of this outrageous fable, an account of the quest for salvation in the pedestrian outer suburbs of Sydney.

At times that comedy overflowed into hate and invective. White himself acknowledged in *Flaws in the Glass* that he was a good hater. And many squirmed when they recognised themselves in those acid portraits of the famous and the infamous that crept into the novels written after he left the seclusion of Castle Hill for the relative hurly-burly of Centennial Park. The notorious cocktail party chatter reproduced in a famous episode of *The Vivisector* had many people, I believe, make anxious telephone calls to their lawyers. Yet the hate, the vicious satire was never — except, perhaps, in *The Memoirs of Many in One* — driven by pettiness or sheer vindictiveness. Yes, he was a good hater, he was capable of wounding, just as he was capable of doing everything to make that dinner party as uncomfortable as possible for at least some of his fellow guests. But there was — and in the books there remains — that intensity, a capacity to see life steady and whole, at least from the perspective from which he was viewing it. He was, in short, one of the last of the romantics. The world does not at the moment take kindly to the solitary artist gazing upon the world from a mountain peak. But it will come to see, I think, that therein resides a source of continuing cultural value.

JAMES WAITES

Manoly Lascaris has just bought a new fridge. The DJs people have taken away the old one (twenty-six years old) and left a brand new one in its place. Bookshelves have been installed for the library of White editions, in many languages, that have been piling up. There's a new vacuum cleaner. There's even a regular house-keeper now; a significant addition to the Spanish treasure whose half day of cleaning and ironing was all Patrick would allow. He and Manoly did the rest. The DJs people have also been in to measure up some new curtains, replacing 'rags' that have been in the house since they moved to Centennial Park from Castle Hill twenty-seven years ago. Friends have pitched in and bought him a television; Patrick had refused to have one in the house.

Manoly has at last had time to see a specialist about his failing eyesight. Is it extravagance? Has the man behind the man that wrote the great books gone mad with the money?

'No,' says Manoly, 'I want to keep the place just like it was when we were living here together. That is important.' It's a way, perhaps, of keeping the partnership alive.

However generous he might have been with others — his substantial estate is being divided up among a range of charities — White was in his own life extremely thrifty. 'There would have been an argument,' says Manoly. '"What's wrong with the fridge we've got?" Or, "Can't it be repaired?" he would have shouted. I put up with that because these things were not important.'

When it came to matters of principle or when

another bust-up with some long and intimate friend threatened, then Manoly stood his ground. Patrick must not make that violent phone call or write that final letter, Manoly would insist. 'He would be furious with me. But the next day he would realise that I was right.' Given the trail of those stung by White's venom, obviously Manoly's wisdom did not always prevail.

But those who knew the pair can confirm the calm, controlling influence Manoly had on White. After White's death, the letters of tribute from around the world rarely failed to mention two key themes. One was regret that the sender had not been able to live up to Patrick's high expectations, sometimes with a brief reference to a noisy falling-out; the other was a tribute to Manoly's enduring patience. Those who had glimpsed the private world acknowledged that White's literary renown was built on the strongest of foundations: the private relationship these two men shared for almost half a century. Unlike many gay couples, theirs was never a secret. Manoly feels no embarrassment, though he was always less outspoken than White. When White in his autobiography *Flaws in the Glass* wrote about their association candidly, he did not show the manuscript to Manoly because he knew he would find it hard to take. It was the only major book Manoly was not the first to see in manuscript form. Even today, while he talks, honestly and affectionately of his life with White, he prefers to avoid the sensationalism White could not always resist.

Manoly goes about the house in a steady, methodical way. Nothing is rushed, and everything is done properly. A glance into his own room and you see bedmaking of a professional standard, combs and brushes lined up on the dresser, a favourite Jim Clifford painting. He is seventy-eight, his hair is thinning, his back a little stooped, always in sneakers because of painful arthritis in the feet.

161

Up early, there is still so much to do. Trips to Bondi Junction twice a week; endless meetings over the estate — this week the State Library is picking up Patrick's desk. There's a siesta after lunch, tea at four and a walk with the dogs in Centennial Park in the afternoon light. The Channel O news, with a scotch perhaps.

After Patrick's death there seemed confusion in Manoly's face. What had been looming for so long, came too quickly. You cannot prepare for the emptiness. But now, with the initial stage of the grieving over, there's more of Manoly's graceful equilibrium and characteristic charm. Even jokes, perhaps even a passing remark about a young man's thighs.

Emmanual George Lascaris was born on 5 August 1912 in Cairo, one of six children; his mother, Florence Mayhew, an American, his father, George, a Greek from Smyrna near the Turkish border. The parents met in Vermont, fell in love and were quickly married. Only then did George, 'the youngest of eight and her darling', write to inform his mother. 'She started creating, and wanted him to come back. He was very much under her influence; and so he came back with his wife and lived with my grandmother in Smyrna.' It was not long before they moved to Cairo, where George set up as a successful cotton exporter. They later moved to Alexandria, which enjoyed a cooler climate.

Then came the First World War, and things started going wrong between Manoly's parents. Much later in life his mother said she 'couldn't stand his infidelity'. At the end of the war Florence went to New York, and did not come back. Manoly was six at the time, his youngest brother only a few months old. His father also disappeared back to America, it was said, with another woman.

'We children were left in Alexandria. There were nurses and governesses in charge; but no one really to look after us.' So the father's two maiden sisters took up the family obligation.

After Smyrna was sacked in 1922 by the invading Turks, the aunts decided to take the children to Athens. However, the family fortune was 'reduced'. 'It wasn't poverty, but people would say, "Poor things — only three maids and a cook to look after all those children." However, it was all right, we didn't lack anything.'

The children loved their aunts. 'I worshipped my Aunt Elly. She was immensely educated. To study my Homer for school I just went up to Aunt Elly and asked, "What exactly did he mean by that?" and she would trot it out, she knew.' She was fluent in French, English and German, though it was her faith in the Greek Orthodox Church, and deep love of its art and poetry, that sustained her. It was the ideal atmosphere for a child of Manoly's sensibility. His own mother was 'very charming, but not an intellectual' and his father's interests 'restricted to sport and women'.

The children's summer holidays were spent in the care of one maid on a small island seven hours by boat from Athens. Aunt Elly would stay in Athens, 'resting and reading'; Aunt Despo, 'more frivolous', would go off to Paris and come back with lots of dresses. It was during Manoly's last such summer holiday, in 1930, that a telegram arrived announcing the father's imminent return. They had not seen him in seven years.

The children were lined up when the boat pulled in. 'He recognised us, counting the number of heads, and waved. After we got into the car I said, "Now the instructions are to take you to a hotel, and I'm coming back to fetch you for dinner." He said, "What, I'm going to a hotel?"'

The aunts had said there was no room in the house. 'I sensed they didn't really want him back, after what he had done to his children, his wife, and how he had ruined their lives. Dinner was very tense. My father didn't even have the head of the table. He sat at the right side of his eldest sister, and was sulking.'

Shortly afterwards Manoly, who was eighteen and had just finished high school, was told he was to sail to Alexandria and join his uncle Mario, then the head of the Egyptian branches of the Bank of Athens. (Manoly's father moved in with the aunts and the other children.)

Manoly began his apprenticeship, staying in Uncle Mario's house. 'It was a tremendous affair, forty rooms and seven bathrooms, twelve servants. It was very rich living. But a trainee at the bank received no salary. My dear Aunt Elly sniffed that I was in difficulty and used to send me a few pounds every so often.'

The apprenticeship over, Uncle Mario moved Manoly to the bank's branch at Port Said because of his skill in languages. 'All these foreigners in Port Said coming off the boats with German marks or French francs or English pounds.' But it was boring, and after about three years Manoly became quite desperate. 'I couldn't really make any proper friends. I was mixed up as a youth. I'd had hardly any experience in sex, and I didn't know which way I was going. Trying to go one way but being pulled the other. You know how it is at that age.'

Even in high school Manoly had a passionate love affair by letter with one of the other boys in his class, though the thought of sex had no part in it. There may have been encounters on the beach at Port Said. But all Manoly will say is that he was 'never promiscuous — all my relationships lasted several years. Before the other one, for the sake of a promotion, had to go off and get married.'

Eventually Manoly returned to Alexandria.

Alexandria in the late 1930s was a city of endless

parties. 'Uncle Mario and his wife were socially at the very top. We were invited to everything.'

In March 1941, Manoly met Patrick White, an Australian with two books already published who had been posted by the Royal Air Force to British air headquarters in Alexandria.

Since Patrick died Manoly has gone over and over the past in his mind, sometimes sharing memories with close friends.

'I had a friend who was a very wealthy Jew, who used to entertain people in the forces. He asked me to a party he was giving because he had an Australian staying. There was no Australian when I arrived. Just all sorts of Alexandrian young men. I knew them all, but none of them was the kind you would waste your time on. Very swish creatures.

'Anyway the Baron had a series of salons in which he would receive his friends. If the butler said, "Come in to the Louis Quinze salon," that meant all the right people, ladies, bankers. He had a Japanese salon for those who were not of the "right society", but because of his inclinations they were his friends.' All of a sudden Patrick appeared through the sliding doors, and all the guests rushed up to him. Except Manoly, who didn't move. 'I stayed at the very end of the room.'

'After a bit, the Baron said, "Shall we go into the Salon Japonais?" I stayed behind, and Patrick stayed behind.'

They introduced themselves, and began a conversation. 'On the way to the Japanese salon there was a rather beautiful painting on the wall of a cardinal, in the Velasquez style. I stopped to look at the painting, because it had that very piercing look I noticed in Patrick's eye. It was the first thing I had noticed when he came in — that's why I held back. Then all of a sudden, when I was looking at that painting, Patrick put his arms around me.' He asked if Manoly would like to see his bedroom.

'It was not romance. It was an attraction through the eyes. I thought to myself when I saw that look: Well, I may have a terrible life, but I must go through with it. Why? I thought that I couldn't escape it. I think Patrick thought the same.'

Manoly soon found a flat for himself, had it reno-vated, and Patrick moved in. They were already seeing each other every day.

In due course Manoly was inducted into the Greek army and sent to Palestine. For the next four years Patrick and Manoly only caught the odd weekend together, sometimes back in Alexandria, or Beirut, or Haifa or Tel Aviv. Patrick's seniority and air force connections made it easier for him to do the travelling, hopping on air force planes or hitching by road convoy. Did those absences add strength to the relationship?

'How I am to tell? If we had stayed together we might have got it out of our systems after the first row. It was always very easy to have rows with Patrick.

'He had already written *The Living and the Dead*. He gave it to me. In those days we were all worshipping D. H. Lawrence, and it gave me the same feeling. A friend commented at the time, "Oh, yes, a very good writer indeed, but you may end up like Mrs Moriarty" — in the book, you know, who gets strangled.'

For company in camp, in Palestine, Manoly bought himself a schnauzer called Franz. Some months later, orders came through that Manoly's camp was moving, and all dogs had to be destroyed. Risking the security of the operation, Manoly contacted Patrick by phone. Patrick flew to Haifa the next day, took a truck to the camp and rescued the dog. In London after the war, Patrick bought three more schnauzers — 'When we came to Australia we would breed them.'

There were always dogs. Later in life it was pugs.

Even today there's a labrador cross, Eureka; Patrick found her ten years ago lying down to die under a tree in Centennial Park. And there's Millie, Manoly's Jack Russell terrier.

At the end of the war Patrick wanted to settle in Greece. But the country was bankrupt, there was a civil war, and how was Manoly to explain the Australian to his relatives? Manoly pushed for a life in Australia he could not have imagined.

Manoly waited in Alexandria while Patrick came back to Sydney to have a look. He wrote back to say it was 'wonderful'. He arrived back in Europe with a completed manuscript of *The Aunt's Story* (much of it had been written on the balcony of Manoly's flat, the rest on the ships to and from Australia). It is a book, says Manoly, that he does not feel close to; it is about the Europe Patrick was leaving behind.

It took several years for Manoly to get to Australia. An entry permit involved in a long wait and the ships were packed with returning soldiers and refugees.

Manoly landed in Sydney in February 1948. 'Patrick was there . . . We had a row straight away, because I gave the porter half a crown.' They found six acres and a bungalow on Showground Road, Castle Hill. Along with a number of established fruit and citrus trees, and a chicken coop, were pigsties which could easily be converted into kennels.

Patrick White had never met a Greek before Manoly, much less one steeped in the ancient rituals, art and literature of the Greek Orthodox Church. Manoly brought with him to Australia seven precious icons given to him by members of his family 'to protect me in this new venture'.

Anyone who has read the books can sense — not least in the frequent triptych structures — the influence of Greek religious art on Patrick's work. 'I never tried to convert him religiously. I spoke about it, and in everyday life you can't help mentioning a few original lines of the gospel . . . ' To this day, if Manoly is ever in trouble, he picks up the New Testament and takes comfort from the Greek that's 2000 years old. 'For me it is definitely literary — it is so beautiful. But you don't believe in all the nonsense, you know.'

Manoly had sold the lease to his flat in Alexandria for quite a good sum, and cashed in some life insurance. Together he and Patrick bought the house in Castle Hill. 'Patrick was supposed to be a poor man in those days. He never, never told me in all his life that he had all this money. People would tell me, he's very rich. I thought he must have blown it before the war in London, Paris, New York.

'Even his nurse told me when I came here. She was the one he loved most, Lizzie Clark. She took me aside and said, "Now you're doing all this work, Manoly, is Patrick paying you very well?" I said, "He doesn't pay me anything, he hasn't got the money." She said, "What? I was there when the will was read. What has he done with all his money?"

Manoly laughs gently as he tells of White's excesses. If the stinginess came from the Whites, the temper, he says, came from his mother's side, the Withycombes. He knows people will wonder why he put up with it. Why then? 'Because we loved each other.'

There was no writing for the first couple of years at Castle Hill. Patrick would 'walk the dogs and milk the cow', while Manoly was gardening. At first it was vegetables, later flowers, though commercially it was always a failure. There were still chickens, fruit trees and cows, so Manoly decided to sell the eggs, oranges and cream. Manoly recalls: 'When Patrick started to write *The Tree of Man* he said, "I can't bear this any more, people coming to the gate . . . when I've got to sit down and write." I said, "How am I to make some money?" "What do you want money for?" Patrick asked. "You've got everything, I feed you." "Well I can't, Patrick, I'm not going to ask you every time I need new shaving blades or a new pair of shorts.'"

Small amounts were forthcoming on Manoly's next birthday and at Christmas. With this Manoly bought a motor scythe and went off to cut grass around the neighbourhood. This meant getting up at 4 am to feed the chickens, and do other farm jobs; then out cutting grass from nine until four; and then back home to chop wood, and more farming chores. 'While Patrick was writing, poor man.'

White would work into the early hours, Manoly staying up to tend the fires and bring in cups of tea. The books did not come easy, and there were rows as Patrick's frustration would overflow.

After an explosion, which would always be more self-hate than hate, and through which Manoly would try to stay calm, Patrick would fall at Manoly's feet, wrap his arms around his beloved's knees, and beg forgiveness. Without Manoly, he would weep, he would be nothing. It was always sorted out in bed. Not just in those early days, but to the end. If people are looking for the secret of why they survived so long, says Manoly, then certainly a successful sexual partnership was fundamental.

If there is a book that has him in it, says Manoly, it's *The Tree of Man*. It has a lot of highs and lows they experienced together at Castle Hill.

Manoly established a business grooming and trimming schnauzers. That worked for a while, until Patrick got restless. '"All those bloody women," he would complain, "they like you to come all the time because they want you." He knew that I wouldn't have done it with any of those women. It was a kind of theoretical jealousy. So I had to give that up.' Manoly laughs again.

When Patrick's mother died in 1963, she left Patrick

a fortune he could no longer hide. 'He completely swung the other way. "Now Manoly, you have been wonderful, I never thought there was anybody else like you", and all that.' Sometimes it's Patrick's own voice you hear when Manoly speaks. They were to move to Sydney, and Manoly was 'never going to have to do any more work, certainly never in the kitchen'.

Patrick bought the house at Centennial Park for cash, and renovations were done: putting bedrooms in upstairs where the attic was, opening out the clutter of rooms downstairs into an attractive living space, spare rooms and a study. Manoly got to work on a sand-dune that is now the garden. They would meet for meals, but when Patrick was writing, Manoly would not speak unless spoken to. 'He had a look in his eye, and I did not break the thread.'

When the Castle Hill house was eventually sold, Manoly's financial situation eased, though Patrick never came good with the promise of a chore-free life. 'It was something he couldn't do, it was against everything.' Even part-time cleaners were at risk: one Russian émigré from Shanghai was thrown out because she had never read any Tolstoy or Dostoevsky. Patrick, Manoly explains, was just looking for an excuse.

Manoly says Patrick was quite undisciplined when they first met. The dull life at Castle Hill, the forced routine of a farm and Manoly's watchful eye made it possible for Patrick to work without interruption. By the time they moved to the city, Patrick had published *The Tree of Man, Voss*, and *Riders in the Chariot*, and *The Solid Mandala* was about to appear. In later years, Patrick was to describe Manoly as his own 'solid mandala', and not only to friends. In his autobiography *Flaws in the Glass* White pays tribute to the 'small Greek of immense moral strength, who became the central mandala in life's hitherto messy design.'

The days at Martin Road, Centennial Park, were

taken up with Patrick writing, Patrick sometimes cooking, and Manoly pretty much taking care of everything else. 'Patrick used to feel he helped. He would point at part of the garden and say, "That needs watering."'

'The house was a home,' says Manoly, 'for people who liked living at home.' The ambience has always been one of relaxed informality. There are paintings everywhere, all Australian — though the best are already with the New South Wales Art Gallery.

The house is in Manoly's care until he dies; then, along with the rest of the substantial estate, the proceeds are to be divided up among four main charities: the New South Wales Art Gallery, the State Library, the Smith Family and the Aboriginal Islander Dance Theatre.

Some have found it odd that after forty-nine years of 'marriage' Manoly has been left comfortably off, but only as caretaker of the estate. In fact, if the house and money had been left to Manoly he would have used it to endow the Centennial Park house as a White museum. Patrick probably knew that, and thought it was something he would not encourage. Patrick ensured that the charities did not lose out to literary posterity — though the property can probably be purchased from the benefactors if someone wishes to put up the money.

Though it's out of his hands, Manoly believes he can at least make his own wishes known. Meanwhile he is determined to keep the place in good repair.

That is typical of Manoly Lascaris — his eye is always on the bigger picture. He knew that in meeting Patrick White he had met his fate. He knew, if he did not keep his cool while Patrick raged, the relationship would have been torn to shreds. He let me read the letters of condolence, 'because someone should know'. He will speak about his life because it is important 'for certain things to be understood'. A biography of White by David Marr was published in July.

It might have been a life in the shadows, but Manoly is his own man too. It has been a life of love and determination, as if seeing a monumental project through. Both Patrick White and the readers of his novels owe Manoly more than can be imagined. A martyr for the cause? Not exactly, though Manoly admits there must have been something of the masochist inside him, and of the sadist in Patrick. 'That, too,' Manoly says, 'had to be satisfied.'

Of the forty-nine years? 'I had to go through with it, as I said. And I did go through with it. It's been very worthwhile and a great experience even though there were moments of great difficulty. The last few years when Patrick was declining, and probably realising that he was going to leave me alone — then he really became quite a different person. He wasn't saying harsh things. Perhaps because he was too weak; or perhaps he thought about it — "I've hurt that man on several occasions I can well remember." I never reminded him.'

A CHECKLIST OF HIS WORKS

(1929/30)   *Thirteen Poems* Privately printed in a very small number (26) for distribution among his family. Only one copy known to exist.

1935   *The Ploughman and Other Poems* Sydney: The Beacon Press, 1935 Illustrated by L. Roy Davies. A limited edition of 300 copies.

1939   *Happy Valley* London: George Harrap,

1940   *Happy Valley* New York: Viking

1940   *The Living and the Dead* New York: Viking
The Living and the Dead London: Routledge

1948   *The Aunt's Story* London: Routledge
The Aunt's Story New York: Viking

1955   *The Tree of Man* New York: Viking
The Tree of Man Toronto: Macmillan
The Tree of Man London: Eyre & Spottiswoode

1957   *Voss* New York: Viking
Voss London: Eyre & Spottiswoode

1961   *Riders in the Chariot* London: Eyre & Spottiswoode
Riders in the Chariot New York: Viking

1964   *The Burnt Ones* (Short stories) London: Eyre & Spottiswoode
The Burnt Ones New York: Viking

1965   *Four Plays* London: Eyre & Spottiswoode

1966   *Four Plays* New York: Viking
(English sheets with US title page added.)
The Solid Mandala London: Eyre & Spottiswoode
The Solid Mandala New York: Viking

1967   *Four Plays* Melbourne: Sun Books
1st Australian edition. Paperback

1970   *The Vivisector* New York: Viking
The Vivisector London: Jonathan Cape

1973	*The Eye of the Storm* London: Jonathan Cape
1974	*The Eye of the Storm* New York: Viking
1974	*The Cockatoos: Shorter Novels & Stories* London: Jonathan Cape
	The Cockatoos: Shorter Novels & Stories New York: Viking
1976	*A Fringe of Leaves* London: Jonathan Cape
1977	*A Fringe of Leaves* New York: Viking
1978	*Big Toys* (Play) Sydney: Currency Press. Simultaneous cloth and paperback.
	The Night the Prowler (Short story and screenplay.) Ringwood, Vic: Penguin Books
1979	*The Twyborn Affair* London: Jonathan Cape
	The Twyborn Affair New York: Viking
1981	*Flaws in the Glass* London: Jonathan Cape
1982	*Flaws in the Glass* New York: Viking
1983	*Signal Driver: a Morality Play for the Times* Sydney: Currency Press. Paperback original.
	Netherwood (Play) Sydney/Adelaide: Currency Press in association with The State Theatre Co of South Australia. Paperback original.
1986	*Memoirs of Many in One* London: Jonathan Cape
1986	*Six Urban Songs* (Lyrics) Written in 1963 and delivered to the composer, Moya Henderson in 1974. Performed in April 1986. 'Night and Dreams' 'Song of the Housewife' 'To Watch the River' 'Rhinestones' 'Sick Song' 'God' Published within the SSO concert programme, April 12, 14 & 15, 1986.
1987	*Memoirs of Many in One* New York: Viking
	Three Uneasy Pieces Fairfield, Vic: Pascoe. Paperback original.
1989	*Patrick White Speaks* Sydney: Primavera Press. Paperback original.
	Three Uneasy Pieces London: Jonathan Cape

JUVENILIA AND UNPUBLISHED WORKS

NOVELS:

1930	*The Immigrants*
1930–31	*Sullen Moon*
1931–32	*Finding Heaven*
1938–39	*Nightside*

PLAYS:

1922	*The Mexican Bandits*
1926	*The Maelstrom*
1932	*Bread and Butter Women* (Performed 1935)
Between 1935 & 1938	*Into Egypt* and at least 2 other plays – titles unknown
1936 or early 1937	*School for Friends* (One act play performed in 1937)
1938	*Return to Abyssinia* (Performed 1947)
(No date)	*Shepherd on the Rocks* (Produced 1987)
1989	*Four Love Songs* Four one act plays written to be performed together

COMPILED BY NICHOLAS POUNDER

NOTES ON CONTRIBUTORS

Phillip Adams is a broadcaster and chairman of the Australian Film Commission.

Franca Arena is a member of the New South Wales Legislative Council.

Veronica Brady is a Loreto nun and head of the English Department at the University of Western Australia.

Edmund Campion is a priest and teaches at the St Patrick's Seminary, Manly. He is the author of *Rockchoppers.*

Manning Clark died in 1991. He was a historian and author of *A History of Australia* in six volumes.

Kay Clayton is a residential care worker at the Anglesea Respite Care Centre

Tyler Coppin is an actor and starred in *The Ham Funeral* in 1989 at the Sydney Theatre Co.

Paul Cox is a film-maker. His latest film was *The Golden Braid.*

Barry Dickins is one of Australia's leading comic writers. He is the author of *The Gift of the Gab.*

Dorothy Green died in 1991. She was a greatly admired poet, academic and critic. Her most recent book was *Reader, Writer, Critic.*

Nicholas Hasluck is a writer whose latest novel is *The Country Without Music.*

Carolyn Hayes-Groves is a writer who teaches at the University of Canberra.

W. J. Hudson is the Editor of Historical Documents at the Department of Foreign Affairs and Trade.

Elizabeth Jolley is a writer whose latest book is *Cabin Fever*.

Barry Jones is a member of the federal parliament and chairman of the Commission of the Future.

Janet Kenny is a Sydney writer.

Elisabeth Kirkby is a member of the New South Wales Legislative Council and is the leader of the Democrats.

Gabrielle Lord is the author of *Jumbo* and *Salt*.

Humphrey McQueen is an academic who has written widely on Australian art and politics.

Richard Meale composed the opera *Voss*.

Finola Moorhead is a writer and author of *Remember the Tarantella*.

Jack Mundey is a political activist and environmentalist.

Nicholas Pounder is a dealer in rare books in Sydney.

Elizabeth Riddell is a poet and journalist. Her most recent book of poetry was *From the Midnight Courtyard*.

Andrew Riemer is an academic and journalist. He teaches at the University of Sydney and reviews literature for the *Sydney Morning Herald*.

Neil Runcie is an economist, president of the Save the Parks Campaign and was a neighbour of Patrick White's.

Clement Semmler is a writer and was head of the ABC.

Peter Skrzynecki is a Sydney poet and author of *The Wild Dogs*.

Frances Thompson is a librarian.

Glen Tomasetti is a Melbourne writer.

Carolyn van Langenberg is a writer and academic who teaches at the University of Sydney.

James Waites is a writer and journalist specialising in the arts.

Chris Wallace-Crabbe is a poet and writer who lives in Melbourne.

Robin Wallace-Crabbe is a writer and painter. His crime novels are published internationally under the pseudonym Robert Wallace.

Michael Wilding is a writer and academic who teaches in the English Department of the University of Sydney.

Ray Willbank is the fiction editor of *Antipodes* and teaches at Memphis State University in Tennessee.

Judith Wright is one of Australia's leading poets whose latest collection is entitled *A Human Pattern*.

William Yang is a well-known photographer. His books include *Sydney Diary* and *Starting Over*.

THE PATRICK WHITE
LITERARY AWARD

Patrick White created the Patrick White Literary Award by a trust deed dated 10 July 1975 which names Perpetual Trustee Company Limited as trustee of the award.

A trust fund for the award was established by Patrick White with the $80,000 he received as winner of the 1973 Nobel Prize for his novel *Eye of the Storm* and a further $20,000 he contributed from his own funds. This money is managed by the trustee to finance the award.

The motivation to establish the award stemmed from Patrick White's feeling that little or no incentive was being provided, either by government or private sponsorship, to encourage the development of Australian literature.

The trust deed directs the trustee to apply the income ' . . . in perpetuity for the purpose of advancing Australian literature by encouraging the writing of novels, short stories, poetry and/or plays for publication or performance by the making of an annual award to an author who has already made a contribution to Australian literature by writing, either alone or jointly with any other person, of published novels, short stories, poetry and/or plays for the purpose of encouraging (him/her) to continue to write such works for publication or performance.'

The award is an amount of cash granted to the winner without conditions. The total amount of the award varies from year to year depending on the income earned by the award trust fund.

The annual recipient of the award is nominated by a

committee of three. The first award committee, formed in 1975, comprised Patrick White, Professor Geoffrey Blainey and James Allison, librarian of the Woollahra Municipal Library.

When a vacancy occurs on the committee a new member is appointed by the continuing members for the renewable term of three years. In the case of a default, committee members are appointed by the head librarian of the Public Library of New South Wales.

Patrick White remained a member of the award committee until his death in 1990. Committee members at the time of writing are Rodney Wetherell of the ABC Melbourne, Joy Hooton, author and academic, Australian Defence Force Academy, Canberra, and Michael Costigan, Sydney, former chairman of the Literature Board of the Australia Council.

The committee is directed to give preference to authors who, in their opinion, have not received due recognition for their contribution to Australian literature. Nominees for the award need not be Australian citizens, or reside in Australia, provided they have resided for a substantial period in Australia.

The following authors have won the Patrick White Literary Award:

1974	CHRISTINA STEAD
1975	DAVID CAMPBELL
1976	JOHN BLIGHT
1977	SUMNER LOCKE ELLIOTT
1978	GWEN HARWOOD
1979	RANDOLPH STOWE
1980	BRUCE DAWE

1981	DAL STIVENS
1982	BRUCE BEAVER
1983	MARJORY BARNARD
1984	ROSEMARY DOBSON
1985	JUDAH WATEN
1986	JOHN MORRISON
1987	WILLIAM HART-SMITH
1988	ROLAND ROBINSON
1989	THEA ASTLEY
1990	ROBERT GRAY

Further information about the Patrick White Literary Award may be obtained by contacting the trustee:

PERPETUAL TRUSTEE COMPANY LIMITED

39 HUNTER STREET

SYDNEY NSW 2000

THIS BOOK WAS PUBLISHED ON

SEPTEMBER 30 1991

IN A LIMITED EDITION
OF 220 HARDBACKS,

20 OF WHICH ARE NOT FOR SALE
NUMBERED I TO XX.

*SIX THOUSAND COPIES
WERE PUBLISHED IN PAPERBACK.*